Lifetime

A TREASURY
of
UNCOMMON
WISDOMS

*A Collection of
Articles from
the Popular
Series by
Maritime Life*

**MARITIME
LIFE**

Macmillan Canada
Toronto

Canadian Cataloguing in Publication Data

Main entry under title:
Lifetime: a treasury of uncommon wisdoms

ISBN 0-7715-9161-6

1. Conduct of life.   I. Kerner, Fred, 1921-
II. Maritime Life (Firm).

BF637.C5L5   1992   158   C92-093091-3

Cover design by Irene Carefoot and Mike Young

1   2   3   4   5   GP   95   94   93   92

Macmillan Canada
A Division of Canada Publishing Corporation
Toronto, Ontario, Canada

Printed in Canada

Printed on paper
containing over 50%
recycled paper including
10% post-consumer fibre.

CONTENTS

III · KNOWING THYSELF

ABOUT THE AUTHORS

Montreal-born **Fred Kerner** has written several dozen books, contributed to scores of periodicals, and written for radio, television, and the stage. He has worked as a reporter with *The Gazette* (Montreal), Canadian Press, and the Associated Press. He worked at Prentice-Hall as a book editor, and is a former Vice-President of Publishing for Harlequin Enterprises. His writing has garnered him many awards, including the Queen's Silver Jubilee Medal. He lives in Toronto.

(FK)

Naomi Mallovy is an award-winning journalist and writer who specializes in health, science, and travel writing. A former reporter with *The Globe and Mail*, she has also been an assistant editor at *Canadian Homes and Gardens*, a copywriter with advertising firm J. Walter Thompson, and a book editor at the Ontario Institute for Studies in Education. Her articles have appeared in such magazines as *Homemaker's*, *Chatelaine*, *Maclean's*, and *Equinox*. She is also the author of *About Face*, a book about women's health. Mother of three grown children, she lives in Toronto with her husband.

(NM)

More than fifty of **Silver Donald Cameron**'s plays have been produced by the CBC, while others have appeared on the stage and on TV. His short stories and essays have appeared in such magazines as *Saturday Night*, *Maclean's*, *Canadian Business*, *Homemaker's*, *The Nation*, and *The Atlantic Monthly*. He has received numerous National Magazine Awards for cultural reporting and travel writing, and his TV drama "Peggy" was voted best short film at the 1991 Canadian Film Celebration. He is also the author of nine books; his most recent, *Wind Whales and Whisky*, was published in September 1991. He and his wife, Lulu Terrio-Cameron, live with their son in a Halifax apart-ment, a renovated home in D'Escouse, Cape Breton, and a twenty-seven-foot sailboat that they built themselves.

(SDC)

Allan Gould is the author of countless magazine articles that have appeared regularly in *Toronto Life, Canadian Business, Finan-cial Times, Chatelaine*. He is a regular contributor to the monthly humour column for Canadian Airlines *In-flight* magazine. He is the author of sixteen books on such topics as profiles of entre-preneurs, cultural history, original humour and political satire, including *The Top Secret Tory Handbook*.

(AG)

Tony Foster is a former CEO, businessman, and airline trans-port pilot. He is the author of thirteen books, his most recent being *Swan Song*, to be released in 1992. He has written numer-ous scripts for film, radio, and for such TV shows as "Border-town." He has also acted on both radio and TV. His latest role was in "Journey into Darkness, the Bruce Curtis Story." He lives in Halifax.

(TF)

After years in New York City publicizing the work of other writ-ers, **Constance Moffit** decided to move to Canada and do some of her own. Her articles have appeared in New York's *Free Spirit* magazine and in the international newspaper *The Vajradhatu Sun*. She is currently writing a romance novel. She is employed full-time as a senior editor at Corporate Communiations Lim-ited in Halifax, where she writes speeches, position papers, annual reports, video scripts, and articles.

(CM)

INTRODUCTION

"SHOW A LITTLE light," a wise man once said, "and the people will find their own way."

During the past two years, we at Maritime Life have been trying through our *Lifetime* column to shed a little light on some of the issues that concern thoughtful Canadians today—issues of health, family life, personal development, and business life. How can I take care of my health when I'm constantly travelling? What should I do about my underachieving child? How can I save time—and what will I do with the time I save? How can I be more creative in every aspect of my life?

We have no magic answers to these large questions, of course, but we're interested in knowing what others are learning about them. We believe that good ideas should be shared, and we also believe that two good ideas rubbed together may spark a third idea that is better than both.

Lifetime was conceived in that modest spirit, as one side of a dialogue with other thoughtful Canadians. But the character of *Lifetime* was also a strategic decision. We realized that everyone today receives torrents of news, advertising, and information. Nobody can absorb it all, let alone evaluate it. Rather than shouting louder to make our voice heard, we thought we might try shouting softer. We wondered whether we could make a stronger impression on the people we wanted to reach if we tried to serve them rather than sell them.

So *Lifetime* was directed not just to our potential customers, but to the whole community to which they belong. And it focused not only on our business concerns, but also on all the roles we play in our lives—parent, consumer, citizen, traveller, and so on. For the same reason, we ran the columns not in the business section of *The Globe and Mail* and *Les Affaires*, but in the general editorial pages, where they would be seen by academics, students, professionals, and public servants, as well as by managers and executives.

A dialogue, by definition, is an exchange of ideas between two parties, and so we recognized that the real test of *Lifetime* would be the reaction of readers. If the initiative worked as we hoped, it would stimulate readers to write to us or call us with their suggestions and observations.

We were not disappointed: the reaction was instant and immediate. Nothing has pleased us more about *Lifetime* than the extent and quality of its readers' reactions. As this book was going to press, for example, we published a column called "Creative Complaining." Within a few days we received hundreds of responses by phone, fax, and letter. Since *Lifetime* began, we've had thousands of responses—and only three complaints. In fact, when we switched to a bi-weekly publication schedule, we received a flurry of concerned faxes on the day the column did *not* appear.

The common thread in most of the responses has been gratitude. People write us simply to express their appreciation for articles that they find perceptive, intelligent, and useful. Many ask for permission to quote from the articles, or to reprint them in other newsletters or bulletins. A number of readers have contacted us to suggest topics for future articles, and on several occasions we have commissioned new articles based on readers' ideas.

Lifetime has thus become a genuine dialogue jumping back and forth beween Maritime Life and the readers of the column. And as a genuine dialogue, it is a genuine success.

Lifetime has served Maritime Life's own purposes as well. Our objective was to become better known to our potential clientele, and to develop a distinctive personality in our market. Life insurance is very much a "people" business—and a fascinating one for those of us who work in it—but for many consumers, unfortunately, the life-insurance industry seems to be one vast, bland blur.

Lifetime has helped Maritime Life to stand out from that grey background. Before we started producing the columns, I often found that new acquaintances were not really sure what Maritime Life was, or what we did. Now they say, "Oh, you're the insurance company that publishes those great little articles . . ."

We are indeed, and we're proud that our company is so closely associated in people's minds with *Lifetime*.

A number of people have worked hard to create this multi-faceted success story and I am heartily grateful to them. Corporate Communications Limited, our public relations counsel conceived and implemented the concept with skill and tact, and continue to successfully manage it on a daily basis.

I am particularly eager to acknowledge the contributions of *Lifetime*'s writers. You will find the author's initials at the end of each article. *Lifetime* articles are a difficult length, and it takes knowledge, skill, and iron discipline to identify an issue, develop an approach to it, and come to a satisfying conclusion—and do it all in not much more than 600 words. One writer recently told me that writing a *Lifetime* article is like doing a crossword puzzle or composing a lyric poem. To do it with consistency, flair, and insight requires superior craftsmanship and talent.

So I am pleased—but not surprised—that the achievement of the *Lifetime* writers has been recognized by two international awards, including a Bronze Award in the 1990 Mercury Awards international competition for excellence in column writing. The Mercury Awards attracted more than 1,000 entries from every corner of the globe. Clearly, *Lifetime*'s writers are world-class.

By their nature, writers are unique and individualistic, and one of the chief rewards of their profession is public recognition. The authors have laboured anonymously without complaint, but I am pleased to acknowledge them here by name, notably Silver Donald Cameron, Fred Kerner, and Naomi

Mallovy, who between them have written the bulk of the articles. The others are Allan Gould, Tony Foster, and Constance Moffitt. Without the curiosity, interest, research, and talent that they and their colleagues have demonstrated, *Lifetime* could never have succeeded.

Because I believe the *Lifetime* articles are of enduring interest, I am happy to present them to you as a collection. I hope you will find them informative, entertaining, and stimulating—not just today, but for many years to come.

J.D. Crawford

J.D. Crawford
President and CEO
The Maritime Life Assurance Company

I

WORKADAY

WISDOMS

☙

COUNTERACTING JET LAG

AN OVERNIGHT FLIGHT to London or Paris immediately followed by an important business meeting—no, not the greatest idea, although many business people must face such a schedule. After a fitful night's sleep, and with their inner clocks all skewed, they're at their lowest ebb, least likely to give their best judgement to pressing problems.

With such agendas, it's no wonder corporations, particularly those with international business, are looking at ways to minimize the effects of jet lag on their executives.

One way to make things easier is to fly business class, particularly on long overnight trips. It makes for a more comfortable and restful trip. When companies have a great deal of overseas business, good rates can often be negotiated. Daytime overseas flights are another alternative. They make it easier to adjust to time zones.

There are advantages to the two-day trip; you can keep on your home time as much as possible and avoid jet lag. But the cost of these trips must be compared with a more fruitful trip of a week or ten days.

Executives agree that the effect of jet lag varies depending on which direction you are travelling. North/south trips have little effect on your internal clockwork because you cross no time zones. Travelling east to west, when you gain time, is less disturbing than travelling west to east, when you must catch up six hours or more, depending on your destination. (You may arrive with that four a.m. feeling and find yourself in the midst of a busy day.) On a six-hour westward time shift, it can take about two days to readjust the sleep/wake cycle, and five days for the body temperature, according to medical experts. During the day you may have to operate with a low, middle of the night body temperature. Studies show that lowered mental activity resulting from jet lag often correlates with a low body temperature.

Hormonal rhythms take even longer to adjust. The effects of jet lag vary; in some people, besides sleepiness and fatigue, it also produces headaches, loss of appetite, and stomach upsets. All the more reason for the timing of programs to allow a buffer period for adjusting to the new time zone. For instance, some corporate planners favour a Sunday night flight before a Tuesday meeting.

Strategies on the plane are important, too. In spite of the plentiful food and drink offered on most airlines, you'll be in better shape when you arrive if you eat lightly, drink plenty of fluids, and avoid alcohol. Also moving around during the flight, walking up and down the aisle or doing some quiet exercises in your seat to keep the circulation going, are recommended. (Foot circlings, knee-bends, shoulder shrugs, or arm presses are possibilities.) And best of all, have a good zzz.

Caffeine in coffee and tea has a role in resetting the circadian clock, depending on when it's drunk. Studies show that in the morning it delays it and in the evening it advances it. This means that before an overnight eastward flight you'd avoid caffeine, but once you'd arrived, you'd go for the black coffee. On a mid-day westward trip you'd skip coffee altogether.

Light also plays a part in adjusting your time-clock. Daylight helps cue you into the new time. It's preferable to get out and about in the daylight of your new destination rather than go for a snooze in a darkened hotel room. Start seeing people, seeing the sights; then, after a good night's sleep, dive into the new business day.

(NM)

cs

The MANNERS *of* MOBILITY

FOR EVERY NEW technology there's a splendid time when the far-sighted owner is entitled, even expected, to show off the new toy. This allows other members of society to share the fun—a few oohs and ahs over "the amazing things they can do nowadays," a couple of insights into the practical applications of the new gadget, and the existential comfort of admiring those romantic figures, those risktakers and innovators, on whom the advancement of civilization depends.

For some time now the cellular phone has enjoyed such attention. Power lunches have been enhanced by the unexpected ringing of a phone from beneath the table linen. Calls taken in shared limos have coincidentally become new business pitches. Vacations have acquired anecdotal clout as the voice of business-to-be-done resounds from ski slopes to the seven seas.

But as the cellular phone becomes more affordable and more ordinary—an essential part of doing day-to-day business in modern times—the intrusions it causes are fast changing from romantic to simply boorish.

By now almost all of us have been present in at least one meeting interrupted by a call on a cellular phone. The receiver of the call does his business without regard to the other people in the meeting, while they sit awkwardly by, trying not to eavesdrop or feel anxious about their own time slipping away. Sometimes trying, too, not to be angry at the disrespect being shown.

A few courteous people have developed private etiquettes for their personal cellular activities. One public relations CEO makes it a practice to use his phone only for outgoing calls. This allows him to use time that might otherwise be nonproductive, without intruding on his clients' time. To make sure that he isn't interrupted needlessly, only his wife and his executive assistant have his cellular number.

Another executive takes incoming calls more frequently but still selectively. If he knows he must receive an important call in the middle of a meeting, he lets his colleagues know before the call comes through that it is important and unavoidable. If no such call is coming, he turns the phone off during meetings.

Busy executives can install "call forwarding" on their portable phones. If they are temporarily unable to take a call because of a meeting, it can be forwarded to an answering machine. A quick check and the call can be returned as soon as the meeting is finished.

One cellular user claims to have modelled her telephone manners on Queen Victoria, whose concern with making her guests feel comfortable was legendary. Once at a banquet with the Shah of Persia, the Queen noticed him drink the water from his fingerbowl; to cover his faux pas, and put him at ease, she promptly raised her own fingerbowl and drank every drop.

The application for cellular phones is obvious. When this executive is in a meeting that is interrupted by a cellular call she uses the opportunity to make a call on her own phone. She claims you can't lose socially with this technique. If persons taking such calls really are boors, they actually do feel more comfortable to see someone else behaving as they do; whereas, more sensitive folk get another message and, without feeling reprimanded, are likely to be more considerate next time.

For now, handling cellular phones seems to be a matter of personal style and choice. But the longer they are mishandled, without regard to the common courtesies of life, the more likely it is that society will find ways to protect itself.

(CM)

‭ℰℐ‬

GOOD HEALTH *at* WORK

MANY COMPANIES ARE looking for ways to promote well-being among their employees because they realize that good health makes for more productive work. Single events like a company golf tournament or a once-a-year marathon (with practice beforehand) are great, but a more comprehensive plan is needed for long-term effect.

Where to start? With the employees themselves, say health promotion experts. "It's important to get everyone involved in thinking about health issues and planning programs," says Professor Anil Verma of the University of Toronto's Centre for Industrial Relations. He suggests forming a task force, made up of different levels of company employees, to recommend health policies. These are discussed and, if practical, approved by management. The resulting programs are received much more enthusiastically than had they been imposed from above.

An alternative to the task force is an ongoing forum in the form of an employee-based committee, which makes recommendations on a continuing basis, and adapts them as circumstances change. Suitable leaders are chosen to carry out particular projects.

The outcome of such multi-level company planning might be a fitness club, a regular lunch-hour jog, the mapping of local jogging or bicycling routes, the setting up of tennis or squash ladders, or baseball teams. When on-site aerobics or regular runs are organized, the company might well decide to provide showers. Recognition and awards provide added incentive to participation.

In the area of nutrition, the group might decide to bring in a dietician once a week to discuss nutritious food or provide special diets for those who request them. (Any pressure to lose weight could be seen as discriminatory.) If there's a cafeteria, the choice of food it provides could be discussed by the committee. A special newsletter, or a page of the regular newsletter, could be devoted to health talk, and posters used to campaign for things like the lowering of cholesterol in the daily diet, the activation of couch potatoes, or the call to butt out.

As in other health matters, a company policy on smoking is most effective when it's a joint decision of management and staff, rather than an edict from on high. The health group may promote drinking in moderation as a general theme, but individual drinking problems must be handled privately, with the person concerned offered counselling.

A more comprehensive program, entitled a "five-year corporate health plan," has been developed by Health and Welfare Canada and already tested in a number of companies across the country. It, too, depends on a representative health committee to help determine the content of the program. This is based on the needs of the employees, determined through a survey of their lifestyles and health practices, the sources of stress they identify at work and at home, and their health and safety concerns. However, critics point out, if such a survey is used, it must be strictly voluntary and anonynmous; otherwise it can be considered just too nosy, an unwarranted intrusion into private lives.

The advantage of a survey-based program, says Health and Welfare's Terence Dalton, is that it determines the current health status of the group, then permits members to tailor their own program to fit their needs. Both physical and social problems at work are identified, so that employees feel they have some control over their environment. Where problems of interpersonal relations are found, a counsellor may be hired or an Employee Assistance Program set up.

The result of such cooperative efforts, it's hoped, is that the workers help themselves to be healthy.

(NM)

≈

GOING IT ALONE

YOU COULD SET your own hours, work from your own home, do only the jobs that interest you. Self-employment would be glorious. Right? Maybe. But before you resign, think carefully. There's no lack of opportunity. In today's economy freelance entrepreneurs are everywhere providing specialized advice, designing clothes, drilling for oil, writing software manuals, doing contract research, appraising real estate. Contract employment, micro-businesses, and temporary-help workers now account for thirty percent of the work-force, and the proportion is rising.

No wonder. Almost every business needs graphic designers, trainers, tax lawyers, technical writers, market researchers, and other specialists. But few can afford to hire them full-time. As big businesses trim corporate overheads and small businesses proliferate, dozens of niches open up for imaginative professionals with the moxie to go it alone.

The rewards can be substantial, but self-employment is strenuous. In *Maverick: Making It As a Freelance Entrepreneur*, Geoffrey Bailey identifies five essential qualities: a need for professional autonomy; a desire for financial independence; a recognition that freelancing is a business; a marketable skill or idea; and an ability to sell.

Freelancers do tend to be specialists and experts—in sports promotion, chimney repairs, fundraising, weapons systems, furniture design, or some other sharply defined area of human endeavour. In good times they invest their profits and take long vacations. In bad times they cash in their life insurance and wake up sweating in the night. Their income fluctuates, but the mortgage, the car payment, and the phone bill arrive with terrible regularity. Successful freelancing requires an iron stomach, ample self-esteem, and a good credit rating.

Despite their specialized skills, freelancers are also generalists who must manage every aspect of their businesses. They promote, propose, make the sales, and manage the project. They create and deliver the product, write up the invoice, collect the money, and do the banking. They buy the equipment, negotiate the loans, juggle the cash flow, deal with the taxman, create the benefits package.

Some freelancers learn these business skills on the job. A background in the humanities or the pure sciences may very well provide unique and highly marketable skills without any practical understanding of the marketplace. Freelancers quickly acquire the necessary street smarts or perish.

Could you survive on your own? Howard L. Shenson's *The Successful Consultant's Guide to Fee Setting* offers some helpful arithmetic.

Start with your present income as an employee—say, $50,000 a year. Then add all the overhead costs that employees take for granted: rent, various forms of insurance (including disability), office equipment and automobile expenses, promotion, retirement fund, legal and accounting costs, and so on.

Overheads normally amount to between eighty and 150 percent of salary. Call it one hundred percent for simplicity. Now add an element of profit—perhaps fifteen percent—which is your compensation for taking the risks and suffering the uncertainties of independent business. The total is $115,000.

To earn that $115,000, you will work 242 days a year—365 minus fifty-two weekends, nine statutory holidays, and two weeks of vacation. Divide $115,000 by 242 and the result is your "daily rate," $460 a day, the amount you'll have to earn every day in order to thrive on your own. Difficult? Yes. But most freelancers welcome the challenge. "I live by my wits," says one of them. "I make my work fit my own needs as a person. I wouldn't want it any other way."

(SDC)

ॐ

ART *in* THE OFFICE

"IT'S THE THING to do." "It's expected." "It shows a level of sophistication." "Having no art is like having no decent furniture." "It's the universal way to treat offices." These are some of the comments from art consultants, art dealers, and corporate executives when asked the reasons for displaying art in offices.

When art is made a part of the office environment it can transform a business-like interior into a dynamic and human space. Though the effect of art is difficult to quantify, it makes a noticeable difference in the attitudes, productivity, and morale of employees. Art means different things to different people, so it stimulates discussion, produces a "flow" that might be absent in more mundane surroundings.

Good art, displayed in reception areas, boardrooms, and corridors, is obviously intended to impress clients and visitors as much as employees. It projects an image of the company. Photographs of the art collection are sometimes used, for this purpose, in annual reports or on Christmas cards. If the collection is extensive, the public may be invited to see it; or a special work may be lent to an art gallery. All this gives prestige to the company, and reveals it as a good corporate citizen.

While aiding the cause of Canadian art, corporations also have tax incentives to buy the art of Canadians, living or dead, since it can be depreciated twenty percent a year as a capital cost allowance, until it's written off. Or, after a period of display in the office, the work can be donated to a museum as a tax benefit. The donor receives the full value of the art at the time of the donation. It takes skill and knowledge to find suitable art for a corporation, and it is chosen in a number of ways. Many

companies employ a corporate art consultant to advise on pur-
chases. In other cases the chief executive officer, or a member of
the firm who is qualified, acts in this capacity. Often the company sets up a committee to make choices, usually on the advice
of an outside art consultant.

The choice of art varies with the corporation. Art consultant
Jeanne Parkin finds that ninety percent of her clients buy Canadian art, usually contemporary, since it is less expensive (though
it may increase in value) and since it is current and of interest.
The focus of a collection, built up over a period of time, may be
abstract painting, multi-media works, or a speciality such as
photography, but must be distinctive to that company. The time
is past when every law office boasted its set of hunting prints,
while other prestigious offices favoured Eskimo carvings, English or early Canadian landscapes, or ships in full sail. More
important there's a desire to latch onto the present and relate it
to the everyday world. This is reflected in a new interest in
photo-based art, in which the photographic image, possibly in a
collage or montage, is crucial to the piece.

Catherine Williams, staff consultant to a bank, as well as several other clients, finds that tastes may run to both representative and abstract art, although she encourages a mixture of both.
She finds it helpful to talk to the employees about art purchased
for the office, to discuss why the artist painted what he did, and
open their minds to new ideas.

Modern, non-representative Canadian art is recommended
by art dealer Olga Korper. In her view it makes the office a place
of challenge and controversy. She finds that two-dimensional art
is more in demand than mixed media, at present.

Smaller offices, without a large budget for art, can rent art
from museums and galleries, or can choose from posters that
offer a wealth of variety and bright images.

(NM)

ॐ

The ETHICS *of* CONSERVATION

BHOPAL, CHERNOBYL, Love Canal, Valdez: disasters such as these have brought world-wide attention to the dangers of environmental damage. Add to the list acid rain, the burning of the Amazon rain forests, the greenhouse effect. Now the risks to the environment that we face seem as great a threat to our security as war.

Surveys show that concern for the environment, which five years ago rated fifth, now ranks first in the value system of the average Canadian. Everybody shares the responsibility; government regulations can only do so much. When it comes right down to it, the health of our environment depends largely on corporate moral leadership, says Graham Tucker, acting executive director of the Canadian Centre for Ethics and Corporate Policy (a two-year-old organization dedicated to helping business, government, and labour make ethical decisions). Only companies that combine ethical foresight, good business sense, and the courage to make the necessary changes will survive, he predicts.

The old react-and-cure-clean-up-afterward method of responding to environmental problems is no longer considered adequate. What's needed is a strong code of ethics for business. The basis of such a code is the concept of sustainable resources, a recognition that the resources of the earth are finite and must be protected and replenished. Such a code, recognized by management and employees, presumes that action to protect the environment will be taken before damage can occur. It advocates prevention, rather than remedy after the fact.

Therefore, a fifth question should be added to those preceding any ethical business decision, says Tucker. The questions are: 1. Is it profitable (market value)? 2. Is it legal (legal values)? 3. Is it fair (social values)? 4. Is it right (personal values)?, and 5. Is it sustainable development (environmental values)?

At a recent conference on ethics and the environment, business managers agreed they must adopt a wider accounting. They must start viewing air, water, soil, and other components of the natural environment as raw materials for which there is a cost and a responsibility. They must look upon pollution control and other measures designed to show respect for the environment as genuine and valuable economic activities, to be reported in the same way as are traditional economic outputs.

Industry has an ethical responsibility to protect the health and safety of people and the environment throughout the lifecycle of its products, it was emphasized. Because industry has more technological capability than individuals or governments, it also has the responsibility to help find practical solutions.

Alertness to international trends can sometimes yield answers. In Sweden, used tires are recycled into road surfacing material. In California, 5,000,000 tires are incinerated cleanly each year (in the absence of air) to produce enough electricity for 15,000 homes. Other uses are as artificial reefs, crash barriers, car mats, bumpers, and hose pipes. Devising such alternatives requires a whole new mindset, a constant consideration of recycling possibilities.

Adherence to "green" principles is not only ethical, it can also offer a competitive advantage as opportunities arise to develop new products and services that are environmentally friendly. By the same token, failure to think green, by all levels of employees, can doom companies to public censure and possible failure. With the new urgency to save the environment, it pays to be good.

(NM)

IF YOU LOVE YOUR JOB

To SOME PEOPLE, their work is a source of great satisfaction. To others it's just time to put in until they can enjoy what they consider their real life after work.

"I love my work," beams Amanda. "I feel so lucky doing what I really enjoy, and calling it work!"

"My work's okay, but I only work so I can have fun in my free time," says Richard.

"I don't like my work, but what can you do?" sighs Gordon.

There are many degrees of satisfaction or the lack of it with work, no matter what kind it is. One person's idea of drudgery is another person's idea of fun and games. Satisfaction at work rubs off in other ways, too. When you feel good about yourself, you're more apt to get a hang out of other things in your life as well. But does this mean that if you're happy at work you do a better job? The experts have been arguing about this proposition for some time, and the consensus is no, at least, not exactly. Although your work may give you a feeling of satisfaction, the fact that you enjoy it may or may not mean that you do it well. There's a little matter of rewards.

If people do good work, they are rewarded by higher pay, promotion, praise from the boss (external rewards), or by feeling pleased with themselves, proud of doing a job well, basking in the approval of others (internal rewards). Although rewards of any kind increase people's satisfaction and spur them on to better work, the internal ones are the more powerful. They increase individuals' self-esteem to the point where they identify themselves with the job and become more involved in it.

There are a few exceptions to this theory. Some people like

their jobs even though they're not particularly good at them, or receive no rewards. They may enjoy the task for its own sake, or enjoy the company of the people they work with. Others get bored or restless, and they may be the type of characters who'd get bored or restless at any job.

What makes people get really turned on to their work? Experts recognize three factors, whatever the job, from assembly line worker to executive.

First, they must feel their job is meaningful, useful, important, whether it be nursing the sick or manufacturing nuts and bolts. It must challenge their skills enough so they don't get bored, and they should be able to see the job as a whole, with visible results (the whole product or service, not just parts of it).

Second, they need to have some responsibility, feel personally accountable for the results of their efforts. This can happen whether they're piling boxes or preparing a sales plan. They can then take pride in doing a job well. It also helps if they have some freedom in scheduling their time and planning their work; it doesn't always have to go by the book. The result is that when work goes well, they can feel it's largely thanks to their own efforts, and get all those nice internal rewards.

Third, they must be able to find out, on a fairly regular basis, whether or not their work is satisfactory. It's especially effective if the feedback comes from the work itself, when they have some way of measuring or counting or gauging its effectiveness.

These are some of the ways of increasing job satisfaction, for yourself or for your employees. Because these methods have built-in rewards, they should improve job performance, too. But how much the satisfaction has to do with it can never be exactly measured.

(NM)

Cℑ

The BUSINESS COACH

BUSINESS IS WAR. Business has a culture. Business is a jungle. A business is a vehicle: you drive it.

Our metaphors shape our attitudes and our attitudes shape our actions. If business is war, then the company is an army—hierarchical and rigid, with divisions and tactics, officers and recruits. In one such company the workers are actually called "mutts" and "grunts"—American GIs' own term for themselves. But the military metaphor may be ill-suited to the fluid, complex, fast-moving 1990s. Armies are often ponderous, imprecise, and inflexible. If we need better organizations, then we need richer metaphors.

Sailing provides a powerful metaphor. Our enterprises navigate steadily towards their destinations through fair weather and storms, tacking and shortening sail in adverse winds, spreading clouds of canvas to a favourable breeze. The successful business, like the successful voyage, requires courage and knowledge, a sound vessel, reliable charts, and a capable, disciplined crew.

The strongest new metaphor is sport: business as a game. A team, like an army, is a structured group, designed to defeat an opponent. Unlike an army, however, a team requires that every player be committed and capable of independent action on behalf of the whole team.

We know how to play effectively together on a softball team, but we leave that knowledge behind when we go to work. Most of us, it has been said, take an absolutely professional approach to our so-called amateur activities, while taking a thoroughly unprofessional approach to our business activities.

17

In sports, the leader is not a boss, but a coach and a guide. He is not out on the ice, actually playing the game. It is Gretzky, not his coach, who makes the split-second decision to shoot, pass, or faint. The coach supports the players, organizes training, recognizes and rewards performance. But the players play the game.

In business the "players" are the people who make the product and deal with the customer. The switchboard operator, the checkout clerk, the customer service representative—these, not the president, provide the customer's direct experience of the company.

How much coaching, training, and orientation do they receive? How is their performance scored and rewarded? Do they feel like players, or just small cogs in an impersonal machine?

Jack Donohue, the ex-coach of Canada's Olympic basketball team, is now a popular business speaker. Donohue tells his audience that a good coach should be a consultant whose role is to induce players to do better than they thought was possible.

"There is a point in our minds where we think that if we try any harder, we will die," he says. "The coach's job is to raise that point."

And if business is a game, then we're allowed to enjoy it. As Robert Townsend says, "If it's not fun, and it's not profitable, why do it?" The great novelist Margaret Laurence believed "that work should be something that you love doing, that you put everything you have and more into it, and that only that kind of work is really worthy of the name."

That joy in work is what we want not only *from* our teammates, but *for* them, too.

(SDC)

꿍

MESSY DESKS

HANGING OVER THE desk of a friend is a large photograph of Albert Einstein's desk as it was found after his death. The caption reads simply: E(nergy) = M(ess) C(onfusion). The desk in the photo is, of course, as messy as any you've ever seen. So is the desk sitting under the photo.

This is not an uncommon phenomenon. There are many well-known people who live with constant mess on their desks—and a standing order to anyone charged with keeping the area clean: Do Not Touch! The list includes Lee Iacocca, Charlton Heston, William F. Buckley, and it could go on to fill the rest of this column. One writer of our acquaintance simply "filed" all his correspondence atop his desk—chronologically as it arrived, with the most recent missives on top. And he had no difficulty finding any particular item he wanted, as long as nobody disturbed the shaky pile of paper.

One former member of the Winnipeg City Council said she worked better in an atmosphere of "organized clutter." But she added, "Nothing sits on my desk longer than six months." The question arises: should a desk always be kept clean or should it merely suit the owner's own work habits? David Wolf, president of Pierce College in California, believes important people have more consequential things on their minds than keeping a clear desk. And who is more important than you?

But if your work capacity is being diminished because you have trouble maintaining an orderly desk—presuming that you want to—listen to a man who can help you do it. He is Jeffrey Mayer and he has developed a consulting business to help people get their desks neat and orderly . . . and keep them that way.

A former insurance firm executive and estate planner, Mayer says he has always looked for easier ways to do things, and has a knack for sorting out priorities "so I can go out and enjoy myself; the idea of work never really appealed to me all that much." Mayer says that sixty percent of the things that sit on a person's desk can be tossed out. And eighty percent of the things in file cabinets can similarly be discarded.

So how do you go about getting rid of the unnecessary paper in your files and on your desk? What you must do, in Mayer's words, is "unclog the thinking process." He sits down with his client and they go through the papers that have accumulated on the desk, one sheet at a time. Mayer asks what each item is and what the client is going to do with it. If it's unfinished work, it's listed on a master list. If the paper is needed, it gets put into a properly labelled file folder. At the end of a couple of hours there are a dozen files at most, a list that may be one, two or three pages long . . . and a garbage can that's filled to the brim, over-flowing and spilling onto the floor.

"There's a beautiful feeling of walking out of the office at night with a nice, clean desk. You know where you are. You've got more control. You know what you are doing as soon as you arrive at work the next morning."

The purpose of the master list, he says, is to give you control of all your unfinished work so that nothing slips through. If you write it down, you don't have to remember it. You can check the list every day and pick off the most important things to be done. When they're done, you cross them off.

Why do papers pile up on a desk? They're there as a reminder of unfinished work, he says. It's a sort of "if I see it I'll remember to do it" approach. Unfortunately, everyone else can see it, too.

Ultimately, the trick of having a clean desk is having no desk at all. And then there are business executives who simply stuff every piece of paper into desk drawers and look as though they're always up to date in their work.

Those of us who are messy know better!

(FK)

꽃

The JOYS *of* SPONSORSHIP

"SHARE THE FLAME."

The words evoke the images: the torch, the red-suited runners, the wine glasses and posters, the pulsing excitement leading up to the Calgary Winter Olympics. And imbedded in all that is the name of the sponsor: Petro Canada.

More than 3,700 North American companies now promote themselves through sponsorship. Fragmenting audiences and steeply rising advertising rates—up to forty-three percent between 1985 and 1989, while the CPI rose only nineteen percent—have driven the value of sponsorship from $590 million to $2.4 billion in just five years.

Lesa Ukman, editor of *Special Events Report*, the Chicago newsletter that tracks the phenomenon, says that sponsorship may be "the next big thing in marketing," the right medium for the 1990s.

"You get a lot of positive, image-building publicity at relatively low cost," says Brian Trowbridge of Far West Industries, the Vernon, B.C., manufacturers of sports clothing. "That's why we're jumping in with both feet this year." Far West has become the clothing sponsor of the Myers Rum All-A-Board windsurfing demonstration tour, which "lets us tag along on the marketing muscle that Seagram's brings to this event."

Sponsorship does indeed represent substantial marketing muscle. Toshiba of Canada, for instance, sponsors 147 events from Vancouver to St. John's. The range of Toshiba sponsorships is astonishing: Canada Day fireworks in Ottawa, Canoe to the Sea in Halifax, a major ski event in Lake Louise (hosted by Ken

Read) for cystic fibrosis, a SkyDome cricket match before 52,000 spectators for the Toronto United Way.

Vice-President Tod Rehm says the company believes in giving something back to the communities where it has been successful. It's a long-term investment. "Toshiba doesn't do anything short-term," he smiles. "We want to be part of the fibre of the community."

The most satisfactory sponsorships are closely related to the target market. Audi has developed a presence in rowing, Volvo in tennis, du Maurier in the performing arts. Tilley Endurables, which aims to make the best adventure clothing in the world, looks for "people who are doing something of great significance," says founder Alex Tilley. People like Joanie and Gary McGuffin, who have both canoed and cycled across Canada, and Toronto grandmother Jane Weber, who will sail in an around-the-world singlehanded race in a boat named *Tilley Endurable*.

"Sponsorship is an advertising investment, not a gift," says Tilley. "But I believe it pays off."

Effective sponsorship requires active participation. Its real value, says Lesa Ukman, is precisely that it provides "a compelling hook on which to hang a promotion campaign." To make sponsorship really pay, she suggests in-store displays, merchandise offers, trade and consumer incentives, and ticket discounts. Shrewd sponsors advertise their association with their events and entertain clients and suppliers at post-event receptions. The windsurfing sponsorship, for instance, gives Far West a legitimate story to tell in news releases, and the finals, in San Francisco, provide an opportunity to wine and dine some key Far West dealers.

The future of sponsorship, like the future of business, is global and sophisticated. An early example may be Amnesty International's "Human Rights Now!" tour, starring rock stars Bruce Springsteen, Sting, and Tracy Chapman—a $12 million sponsorship by Reebok, the British athletic footwear company.

Did the tour sell running shoes? Not directly, says President C. Joseph LaBonte, but "it fit with our values and will live on with the young people who have made our company successful."

Share the values. Share the flame. And share the future.

(SDC)

⁓

COMMON SCENTS

THE PLEASURE OF sweet odors is well-known to everyone. One whiff of some pungent perfume can sometimes make the strongest will a little more pliant. As with anything we tend to take for granted, however, there is a new realization that appealing scents can be used in a variety of ways.

The Japanese manufacturer of cosmetics, Shiseido, has taken a page out of the book Muzak created some fifty years ago. Muzak conceived the idea of using music to motivate and encourage captive listeners as they went about their daily activities. The system proved effective during World War II in factories creating material for the armed forces. There are many manufacturing plants today that play specially selected music to spur on workers. You're bombarded with melodies every time you step into an elevator. And, anathema to many, you are "entertained" almost every time you are put on hold by someone at the other end of a phone call.

Shiseido claims to have discovered scents that, when pumped through the air ducts in office buildings, will "energize and relax" workers. In the morning, the workers will be treated to the pleasantly pungent smell of lemons to fire them up. By noon, the citrus will give way to the sweet scent of roses, with a resultant calming to help the workers digest their lunches. Then, to lift fatigue by mid-afternoon, a whiff of tree-trunk oils will be wafted through the offices. It's all part of a new pseudo-science called "aromatherapy."

The Japanese say jasmine pumped through a hotel air-conditioning system will soothe the travel-weary guest. Your next business meeting might be laced with lavender to lessen mental fatigue. A light floral scent is said to cut by twelve percent entry errors made by computer operators, and the alluring aroma of cinnamon in the reception area will induce calmness. Among positive applications of aromatherapy yet to be discovered could be ways to stop you smoking and drinking, or even assist in the learning process.

Along with what could be the positive side of scent-therapy, there is a darker aspect. That, says Dr. Alan Hirsch of the Smell and Taste Treatment and Research Foundation in Chicago, could be a "subliminal odor technology," which could be used to mislead consumers into buying things they don't want. Not that such methodology—intentional or not—isn't in play today. The smell of freshly buttered popcorn in a theatre lobby can be irresistible. And the fast-food outlets in large shopping malls deliberately waft about Essence of Burger-and-Fries to induce a pang of hunger in all but the hardiest resister of unwanted calories. The same effect exists in supermarkets. A bake shop in the store perfumes the air with the smell of freshly baked bread—a bouquet that many people find hard to resist.

Odor disguising is becoming common. Even perfumes are being masked in department stores. Rather than allowing a proliferation of flowery scents to create a confusion in your nostrils, the unopened packages containing those expensive perfume vials are sprayed with the reassuring scent of . . . baby powder!

What Dr. Hirsch fears is that behaviour can be affected by odors our noses can't consciously detect—in other words, subliminal smells. If the smell of lavender is a gentle mood-lifter, what effect might this have if you are shopping for a new car? Relaxed and trusting, are you more likely to make your purchase from that dealer and regret it later? The potentialities are endless and eventually may require legislation controlling subliminal odor technology.

Meanwhile, be prepared for a raised eyebrow and a

questioning look when you arrive home from the office bathed not in your usual smells of office dust and exhaust fumes, but with the sensuous aroma of jasmine or the pervasive perfume of pine.

(FK)

PROTECTION of
INTELLECTUAL PROPERTY

PEOPLE WHO WRITE a book, invent a manufacturing device, discover a new drug, or write a new computer program are among
those needing protection for their creations. They need patents
to protect the ideas behind their innovation; copyrights for the
expression of their ideas in print, film, records or other media;
and trademarks for the symbols that represent them.

The need becomes obvious when you consider the rampant
piracy of ideas, scientific discoveries, and inventions. And with
Canada now joining other countries in a global economy, it is all
the more necessary to protect our technological and intellectual
advances.

In 1988, major changes were made to the outdated Copyright
Act and Patent Act; but with the rapid pace of development,
particularly in such areas as communications, computer software, and biotechnology, continual revisions are necessary. Fur-
thermore, many details of enforcement and policing of the act
need to be worked out.

The copywriting of material in books and magazines is an
example. It is now illegal to copy from them without payment,
yet people continue to copy pages freely in libraries, schools and
universities, offices and commercial establishments. Also, material is often copied onto data bases without payment of copyright fees. A mechanism does exist for the collection of these
fees. The Copyright Act has approved the use of collectives for
the work of writers and visual artists (photographers, illustra-
tors, and others). But the means of regulating them has not been
finalized.

Libraries are still lobbying for single copy exemption to the fee, whereas the writers and artists favour a minimum fee paid to the collectives for each copying machine, to cover its myriad users. Meanwhile, some blanket licences with federal and provincial government departments are being obtained. These would cover the use of writers' and artists' works in education and in normal government business.

Although computer software is covered by the new act, the protection is not sufficient to prevent many acts of piracy in this rapidly evolving field. The copying of software programs is commonplace both privately and commercially. (In the United States it's estimated that the sale of illicit copies of brand-name programs costs American firms two to three billion dollars a year.) Obviously better coverage and enforcement are needed.

In Canada, patents are only allowed on micro-organisms and other unicellular material, not on plant or animal variations. To be competitive with the United States, where such patenting is allowed, changes will have to be made.

The great expense of research and development by business, government, and the academic world underlines the need for intellectual property rights. If a new product, drug, or process is developed at a cost of millions and then promptly copied, the incentive, and in fact the wherewithal, for research is lost.

In the academic world, a few ethical questions are still unanswered. What degree of collaboration is possible between universities and industries without damaging the freedom of scientists to share their knowledge with their associates worldwide? In some cases secrecy must be maintained, and publication of findings delayed a year or more while patents are awaited. There is also the question of whether ownership of the patents should be in the hands of the university or the business.

Nationally, the necessity for patent copyrights is urgent. "The ownership and exploitation of intellectual property is increasingly viewed as a strategic weapon in the international economic battle, especially in high technology industries," according to a recent discussion paper published by the Science

Council of Canada. Knowledge is power, and the ownership of it a means to create wealth, individually and nationally.

Widespread awareness of the need for intellectual property protection is essential so that the work of individuals can be protected, and the national economy remain competitive.

(NM)

∽

YOUR PUBLIC FACE

WHAT IMPRESSION DO people have of your company? Efficient, thorough, dynamic? Or do they feel that your organization is uncaring, sloppy, perhaps even inefficient? And what contributes to that perception? Undoubtedly, the product or service supplied is a key factor in determining what customers think. But what about everyday etiquette, pure politeness, common courtesy? What is the first thought, for example, people have when they reach your telephone switchboard, or when they come to your reception desk? Is the treatment casual, cavalier, and careless? And if it is, do you feel that it really doesn't matter?

A company president we know manages to check out his company's "public face" a half-dozen times a year or so, much to the company's benefit. When he's out of the office during business hours, for instance, he gets into a phone booth and calls in. He counts the number of rings before the company operator answers the phone. (More than three rings is a no-no.) He manages to disguise his voice so as not to be recognized, and checks out the manner of response of the employee answering.

At other times, in the office, he manages to find a way of walking by at an appropriate moment so that he can listen and watch unobtrusively how people are greeted at the reception desk. In that way he gets a quick snapshot view of how people react to their reception when they visit.

What does this do? Most important, it assures him that his company's public image is one of attention, friendliness, and respectfulness to both current and potential customers.

With the current state of the country's economy, there's a lot to be gained by such tactics. This man has been doing it for decades, and his company has thrived through economic ups and downs.

The company's telephone operator has been trained to recognize the voices of callers. By the second call, usually, the caller is addressed by his or her name. It's always "Mr. Doe" or "Ms. Roe." Frankly, it's a pleasure to phone his office.

These often-forgotten amenities are something the great majority of telephone-sales operations in this country could well afford to revive. Nothing turns off so many potential customers as the "cold call" that immediately turns to a first-name approach. The reaction at the receiving end of the call is, all too often, "Do I know this person? Who does he think he is addressing me that personally?" The usual result: a quick end to the conversation.

Attention to personal details, politeness, a warm attitude—these make for a business atmosphere conducive to success. Anyone who has ever been involved at the sales end of a business is well aware that brusque treatment of the potential customer is a turn-off. Obviously, it's no different with the established customer.

The extra moment it takes to be pleasant pays off in multi-fold fashion. The I-couldn't-care-less "disattention" can add up too quickly to falling results and failing business. The way in which you present yourself, and the company you represent, to the outside world should be the same as the way in which you should act towards co-workers at whatever level. We all want to be treated with respect, treated as intelligent humans, able to live and work in harmony with those around us.

It costs no more to behave in this fashion.

(FK)

RETROPHOBIA

MANY PEOPLE RETURNING to the workplace after a considerable absence suffer from fears and worries. The returning workers may have taken early retirement and found it boring. They may have had the opportunity to take a sabbatical, or a long-needed and lengthy vacation. Many mothers (and in recent years more and more fathers) have taken time to start raising a family.

In the past, no matter what the reason for the layoff, the prospect of rejoining the work-force was usually a time for rejoicing. But the pressures of employment—and especially re-employment—have changed. The emotion felt by the returning worker today is all too often one of recoil.

It apparently makes no difference who they are, what level of responsibility they had or will have, or even the cause of their long layoffs, the reaction is almost always the same. Dr. Davis Lewis, psychologist for Manpower, a major British-based job placement agency, was struck by the realization that there was a commonality of apprehensions experienced by many would-be "returners." In seeking to determine complaints the jobseekers had, Dr. Lewis began to notice a pattern of common fears and problems emerging. It wasn't a phobia discussed in any of the textbooks, so he decided it needed to be characterized. He's called it "retrophobia," a word that seems destined to enter the language permanently. The term refers to all the irrational fears experienced by people when they face the prospect of rejoining the work-force.

As he studied the phenomenon further, he discovered that retrophobia has a number of components. These are:
- Technofear—the terror of modern office equipment.

- Fitting-in fear—the worry about not getting along with colleagues.
- Responsibility fear—a deep-seated angst about making a serious mistake.
- Keeping-up fear—a feeling of foolishness because everyone else seems to be working faster and more efficiently.

"These fears can be overcome," Dr. Lewis said. "Unfortunately, however, many people who are thinking of going back to work feel as though their problems are insurmountable. They build them up in their minds until they become a barrier. The result is that they are then stopped from doing anything about their problem. The more they think about the problems, the greater the problems become."

Retrophobia is like any other fear, the London psychologist points out. "It can be overcome by talking to other people and analyzing the component parts of the panic."

Dr. Lewis is continuing to work closely with the Manpower agency to help people get over their anxieties by showing them what they need to do to cope, and how they can banish the back-to-work bogeyman. He is convinced that the main obstacle retrophobes have is simply getting them to talk to someone else. "If we can only get people to take the first step to talk to someone who understands the problem, they'll find that they are not alone in this experience," he adds.

It becomes a matter of building up confidence. And, he suggests, if you're plagued by technofear, fitting-in fear, responsibility fear, or keeping-up fear, you should consider easing yourself back into the work-force as a temporary worker.

"Many people find that 'temping' is a good way to regain their work habits because it gives them greater flexibility than permanent work." It's proving to be the best way of easing the "returner" into a working routine . . . gently.

(FK)

cs

The WRITE STUFF

PRESIDENT ROOSEVELT WOULDN'T accept it. The year was 1942, and some bureaucrat had cranked out a directive that read:

"Such preparations shall be made as will completely obscure all Federal buildings and non-Federal buildings occupied by the Federal government during an air raid for any period of time from visibility by reason of internal or external illumination."

"No," said FDR. "Tell them that in buildings where they have to keep the work going, to put something across the windows."

The cost of vile prose is sometimes obvious: the ill-drafted directive that creates mistakes and confusion, the clumsy memo that loses an order or spawns a lawsuit, the pompous form letter that enrages a customer. But the heaviest costs are missed opportunities, demoralized people, and poor decisions, or no decisions at all.

Fuzzy language obscures reality and inhibits action, often deliberately. Phrases like "structural adjustments" allow economists to overlook the miseries of bankruptcies and lost jobs. Nobody likes to cut budgets; if we talk instead about "strategic reallocation of resources" we can pretend we're doing something else. The military phrase "collateral damage" evokes a smash-and-grab at a pawnshop, not the reality of broken human bodies. But fuzzy writing more often masks the absence of thought. Productivity, writes a hospital administrator, is the design and implementation of improved systems to maximize output within the constraints of available input. Really? Stripped of its clutter, that sentence does have a meaning, but the meaning is banal. No matter: who will bother to decipher it?

Clear writing reflects clear thinking. It leads to action. A good memo answers three questions: What are the facts? What do they mean? What do we do about it? That's why Procter and Gamble requires one-page memos. The restriction forces managers into short words, short sentences, clear ideas, and concrete proposals.

What can we do to improve business writing? Here are some hints from professional writers:

• Think much and write little. What's your central point? Buttress that point with arguments, refute counter-arguments, draw your conclusions but don't ramble, and don't ever lose sight of that main point.

• Analyze your reader. Who will read this? Customers? Shareholders? The boss? What does the reader know, and what should she or he want to know? What tone should you convey? Decide whether to be warm, informative, or stern, and make sure your words come across that way.

• Start with your conclusion. Don't make your reader puzzle over your purpose. State it right away, and say what you want from the reader. Then give the details and the arguments.

• Be yourself. Say your piece plainly and confidently. Seek clarity, not dignity. An inflated style is full of hot air.

• Use visual aids. Italics, boldface, and "bulleted" lists show the reader how your piece is organized.

• Say it aloud. You would never say, "Yours of the sixteenth inst. to hand, we beg to advise that relevant documentation is enclosed." You'd say, "Here's the report, John." If your work sounds stuffy and stilted when you read it aloud, it will read that way, too.

• Write quickly and re-write. Race through your first draft; then criticize it viciously and revise it. Follow Jonathan Swift's advice: blot out, correct, insert, refine, enlarge, diminish, interline. Polished writers are diligent re-writers. The ability to communicate well is among the most prized of business skills. If you want that skill, you can have it. Good writing comes less from talent than from hard work. And hard work is something that anyone can do.

(SDC)

ॐ

PERSONAL &
BUSINESS ETHICS

ARE THE VALUES of our private lives and of the working world so
different? Often they are the same, which gives us a comfortable
feeling of integrity. Both, after all, reflect the values of the society we live in, and if values change in one area, they're likely to
change in the other.

With the impersonal nature of big-city life, the place we work
has become the community for many of us, somewhat like a
larger family. We spend a great part of our lives at work, and the
influences there are strong. As a result, the values expressed at
work, the sense of responsibility or lack of it, are inevitably
carried over into our private lives.

But what if your own values and principles are at variance
with those of the people in your business? You can then face a
great deal of stress, if not a schizophrenic situation, says Michael
Yeo of London's Westminster Institute of Ethics and Human
Values, and a lecturer at the University of Western Ontario's
Faculty of Engineering. For your own peace of mind, it's essential to maintain a sense of integrity and wholeness in your moral
values, not to split your roles at home and work.

One way to avoid this mismatch of work and private values is
to check out a company before you seek employment there.
Does it deal, directly or indirectly, in products of which you
personally disapprove? What is the reputation and style of the
company regarding management and labour practices, client or
customer relations, or conservation?

It may be only after you've been there some time that you
begin to question some of the business practices of your company. Where do you draw the line between wining and dining

prospective clients, now an accepted practice, or offering them expensive trips or gifts? What if the company is seriously polluting the environment and doing nothing to remedy the situation? What if you run into what appears to be outright dishonesty? Depending on the circumstances, you can report it to the appropriate authority. But first discuss it with the person(s) involved, in case you are mistaken. Also be clear about your own motives, particularly if you are in competition with them, says Yeo.

When the principles of a corporation or a profession are defined in a formal code of ethics, it clarifies thinking about business practices and gives positive support to honest dealings. Codes of ethics, which are becoming more common, not only polish the image of a company, but give all employees a clear idea of what's expected of them. When updated regularly, they can clear up grey areas where conduct is up for question.

It all adds up to a workplace that is more like a family, where common values are espoused, and consideration for others has a high priority. The principles of "Do unto others in the office as you would have them do unto you" and "Do unto customers as you would have them do unto you" are proving that the Golden Rule not only works well in the office community, but pays off in the long run in customer loyalty.

To take these principles a step further, as one executive of an international corporation put it, "Business leaders have to see the bottom line as a means to a community and social end rather than an end in itself."

With such attitudes, employees can feel good about themselves, and have the satisfying feeling that they're working in a good cause. There need be no contradiction between personal and business ethics.

(NM)

COMMITTEES THAT WORK

WE LIVE IN a society that tends to work through committees. Serving on a committee, especially in a business context, is often a necessary part of our employment. When we sometimes form a "committee" in a home situation, we usually do so to develop awareness in the younger generation of what it means to work together as a family.

It is usually in the volunteer organization, however, that the problems inherent in committees arise. And it's in such volunteer situations that most of us tend to get involved. It's rare, if you belong to a service organization of any kind, that you won't be asked to serve more actively than you have, or want to, or even expected to. Yet volunteer organizations must fully exploit the democratic way of seeking consensus. And being of a voluntary nature, they must call on members rather than on a proliferation of paid staff to do the work.

Of course, it's flattering to be asked to serve on a committee. Most of us are inclined to accept, for a variety of reasons: some self-serving, others for the greater good of the greater number. The major question you should ask yourself if you are approached is "Am I prepared to give the necessary time to serve the committee, and the group, fairly?"

It takes a clear sense of personal direction and a strong sense of security to turn down such an invitation. So if you are asked, here are some factors to consider: don't accept unless the work the committee does is something you believe in; and if you do accept, restrict your contribution to the area of your expertise and delegate time-consuming chores to paid committee assistants or willing volunteers whenever possible.

If you are inclined to accept an invitation to serve, you should first understand some of the basic elements of what makes a committee work successfully:

• Each committee member must have definite responsibilities. It is essential that goals be set—a committee that isn't expected to produce a substantial result usually won't.

• Time limits should be set for work to be completed. If the project is a multi-stage one, periodic reports should be made to the powers-that-be.

• It makes good sense to rotate membership on standing committees periodically. In that way there is a steady flow of ideas. Rotation is also a good idea in that it breaks up stagnant thinking patterns. In establishing a rotation, it is also advisable to balance membership on the committee between experienced participants and relative newcomers.

• The level of cooperation of committee members should be reviewed. A committee dominated by one member often produces insignificant results as well as frustrating the other members.

• If committee proposals are rejected by the executive body, reasons should be given for the rejection. On the other hand, if they are accepted, the proposals should be implemented immediately so that the committee can see the effects of its efforts.

Finally, a word about committee size. John Ben Sheppard, a former attorney general of Texas, once surveyed thousands of service groups and discovered that the ideal committee, in his words, "consisted of three-and-one-half people." In other words, the committee that gets the most work done will usually have no more than three members; four is a tolerable number, but just barely.

From sad experience, we can tell you those words were wisely spoken.

(FK)

READING THE CUSTOMER

CUSTOMER SERVICE HAS become the focus of business in the 1990s. Everything in our business, we say, depends on a satisfied customer. Indeed, the only reason to be in business is to find and keep a customer.

But has customer service really changed? Or have we simply developed new ways of making the same old mistakes?

We take seminars, and we learn to smile while we answer the phone, knowing that the act of smiling will enhance the tone of our voice. We introduce ourselves to the customer by name, maintain eye contact, speak positively and enthusiastically, follow up when we say we'll follow up, and communicate if we're delayed. This all seems very laudable. But then we walk out into someone else's premises as a customer. They treat us exactly the same way and it rubs us the wrong way. Why?

The problem is simple, but fundamental. First, personal service is not always appropriate and in the wrong setting it becomes an irritating mannerism. We don't want "relationship selling" at a movie box office: we simply want our tickets. Anything more than a pleasant smile and a "Thank you" is superfluous.

Second, personal service always rings false unless the service really is personal. The animating force of personal service is a genuine interest in the individual customer and his needs. It need not be deep or durable, but, at least briefly, it must be real.

Top salespeople, of course, have always known this. A first-rate real estate agent, for instance, spends a good deal of time with the clients, discreetly probing their financial situation, learning what features of a house really matter to the family and appraising their reactions to the houses she shows them. She listens carefully, nudging them towards realism, helping with the financing, and generally approaching the sale as an exercise in problem-solving for people she knows and likes.

When they finally close the deal on their new home, she genuinely shares their pleasure and satisfaction. She stops by later, when she's in the neighbourhood, just to see how it all worked out. The relationship pays off first in human warmth and enjoyment, but its natural by-products are referrals and repeat business.

The heart of customer service is providing what the customer needs and wants—and that means paying attention to the customer. The techniques only help if they are grounded in the realization that customers are individuals who must be approached individually, and whose needs may differ from one occasion to the next.

The best service "reads" both the customer and the context, and responds appropriately. If one customer is drumming his fingers and glancing at his watch, he's pressed for time: serve him fast. The next customer may be distracted and uncertain. Probe gently to find the reason, and then assuage her anxieties. A third customer may want a leisurely review of models and options. Take your time, and show off your hard-earned product knowledge.

The best customer service is not rooted in tricks and techniques. It consists of one human being responding sensitively to another's needs. When that happens consistently, day after day, businesses build phenomenal consumer loyalty, which they so richly deserve.

(SDC)

CREATIVE COMPLAINING

IF THE PRODUCT doesn't work, or if service was poor, then do us all a favour. Complain. Your complaint will be heard, because managers know that only four percent of dissatisfied customers ever complain. Most unhappy clients just walk away forever. If one person complains, many other voters, clients, or customers are out there in the community, grumbling to their friends. So a handful of letters has a powerful impact.

"If we get ten letters on an issue," says Pat Wilson, community affairs manager at Eaton's head office in Toronto, "it's a very big concern." Politicians are similarly sensitive. Most letters to the Prime Minister are handled by his correspondence unit. The Prime Minister gets a regular scorecard, and a letter on a contentious major issue like Meech Lake or the GST will at least be tallied. A particularly thoughtful and well-reasoned letter on a specific point, however, can make it right through the system and receive his personal attention.

Good managers are grateful for complaints, which they see as opportunities rather than problems. Customer-service trainer Jim Moran compares complaints to the irritating grain of sand that infiltrates an oyster: rather than expel the sand, the oyster shapes a pearl around it.

A good service-oriented executive shapes the pearls in two different ways. First comes the individual customer. If we've really messed up, how can I regain that customer's confidence and loyalty? At a minimum, I can apologize and extend our thanks for telling us about the problem. For minor problems, a complete and sincere apology will often be enough. Beyond that, perhaps we can offer a gift—no charge for the meal, a free night in the hotel, samples of our product. Pat Wilson of Eaton's has been known to send a dozen roses to a disgruntled customer, or to buy dinner for two in a fine restaurant.

The executive's second response eliminates the problem that created the complaint. Jim Moran cites the example of Wil Willemsen of Sunripe Farm Markets, a widely admired small business in Sarnia. When a customer complained of slow service in the bakery, Willemsen asked other customers. They agreed. Willemsen and his staff immediately converted the bakery to self-service, and sales rose twenty-five percent in ten days.

So complaining can be a creative activity. A good complaint solves your problem, prevents future problems, and also benefits the organization that failed you. But what makes a good complaint? Here are some hints from people who handle complaints every day:

• Complain to the top. If you write to the president, he'll pass it down to the highest appropriate executive. If you complain to a lower-level employee, the complaint may not be passed up to the boss, particularly if the employee is worried about being blamed for the problem.

• Be polite, but passionate. You're hurt, angry, or insulted: that's why you're complaining. It's fine to let those emotions show, but keep them under control. Don't be sarcastic or insulting. You want sympathy and action, not defensiveness and irritation.

• Tell the truth, and be fair. If your complaint is valid, you needn't exaggerate. Just give a clear, concise account of what happened and remember that there are two sides to the story, however unlikely that may seem to you.

• Suggest reasonable solutions and acceptable compromises. Your aim is not the public flagellation of the president; you just want the company to apologize and set things right. Tell them what it would take to do that.

You also want to know that the problem won't recur, so ask

about that. In a small way, you're trying to make the world a trifle less frustrating, a touch more efficient and humane. That's the real value of creative complaining.

(SDC)

II

HEALTH'S

WEALTH

 ❧

❦

EATING & STRESS

STRESS CAN CAUSE you to overeat or to not eat enough. You hold the trump card when you know exactly what and when to eat to control your stress. You've seen some people stuff themselves on donuts, candy bars, or cookies when the pressure gets to them. They turn to food as others turn to smoking or drink, as a fix, to ease their stress. That's okay if they don't overdo it, but with many it can become a reflex. You see the results in excess poundage. Also common are those whose busy, stressful lives prevent them from eating properly. They skip breakfast, miss lunch, or simply grab a quick snack, then work through till a very late dinner. Some get so uptight under pressure that they can hardly eat at all.

According to nutritionists, the body is best prepared to handle stress if it has adequate stores of all nutrients, supplied by fruits, vegetables, proteins, grains, and milk products. Although the pressure of work may sometimes make it difficult to find time for them, regular and nutritious meals do much to reduce stress. Until recently, the role of food in controlling our minds and moods has been strictly conjecture. Most people have their "comfort foods," be they mushroom soup, chocolate cake, or peanut butter sandwiches, choices that often date back to childhood conditioning. But now scientific research has shown that the presence and activity of the brain's chemicals that regulate stress can be controlled by food intake. "The dietary changes affect the chemistry of the brain, which in turn affects behaviour," explains Carol Greenwood, an assistant professor in the Department of Nutritional Sciences at the University of Toronto.

It's been found that an increase of the neurotransmitter serotonin in the brain tends to have a calming effect, to mitigate stress. A high carbohydrate meal increases the synthesis of serotonin.

On the other hand, an increase of the amino acid tryptophan, produced by proteins, has an opposite effect; it makes the brain more active. The corollary is clear: if you want to remain alert, eat high protein meals, particularly at breakfast and lunch (fish, chicken, lean meat, eggs); if you want to relieve stress and relax, particularly in the evening, opt for carbohydrates (potatoes, pasta, pie). By the same token, a carbohydrate snack, say in mid-afternoon, can do much to relieve temporary stress.

Managing Your Mind and Mood Through Food by Judith Wurtman, a research scientist at M.I.T. in Cambridge, Massachussets, emphasizes that food does have the potential to make you feel better when you are upset, worried, anxious, angry, frustrated, or tense. "Food is among the most effective and safest of all stress relievers," she explains, "better than cigarettes, alcohol, or tranquilizers, all of which are potentially harmful."

When you eat carbohydrates it takes the pressure off long enough for you to deal more rationally with the cause of your stress. It's important that it be carbohydrates alone (starches and/or sugars), without protein or fat, Wurtman advises. For a quick stress fighter, a small amount, about thirty grams, will do. In several minutes you should feel more relaxed. The carbohydrate "dose" can consist of a few crackers, cookies, rice cakes, a muffin or a plain bagel (no butter or cheese), dry popcorn or candy, depending on how many calories you can afford. Or drink your carbohydrates in the form of herbal tea with sugar, hot chocolate made with water, or a can of caffeine-free regular soft drink, sipped slowly through a straw. Within minutes your stress should ease. Experts agree that a certain amount of stress helps you perform well. With a judicious use of high protein, low-fat meals when you need to be at your peak, and carbohydrates when you need to relax, you are able to regulate the amount of stress you can live with.

(NM)

The GREAT KILLER

WHAT IS THE greatest killer of our time? The question came up in a casual conversation with a family doctor. The answer offered was startling: suicide!

"Suicide? Not likely! The statistics—," we started to say.

"Forget the statistics," the physician interrupted. "I'm not talking about the 'official' definition of suicide—guns, hanging, wrist-slitting, overdosing. Most people develop a much slower method of killing themselves, but one that's just as effective. I'm talking about worry, pessimism, fear. They're the greatest killers of our time."

The fact is that the hectic tempo of today's living, with its resultant tension, is a serious national problem. Canadians, by the tens of thousands, are killing themselves with the most deadly weapon humankind has ever inflicted upon itself: anxiety. Anxiety about business, anxiety about personal relationships, anxiety about almost everything.

Ailments brought on by negative thinking account for more debility than all other diseases combined. The afflictions are not imaginary. They are as real as a broken leg or the flu, as real as electricity, and perhaps as difficult to understand.

How do you combat anxiety, worry, and fear, especially in the face of constant exposure to headlines in the daily press or the nightly newscasts? Whether it's page one or the business section, the editorial page or the Op-Ed page, "The Journal" or "W-5," the making of emotional upset is ever-present.

If people expect the worst that's what they usually get. Negative thoughts always produce negative results. Once you've lost the confidence that things will go well—lost faith in yourself—

you are short-circuiting both your health and your ability to cope with life's problems.

Medicine has proven conclusively that the mind and the body are interrelated; what affects one, affects the other. William James, the noted American psychologist, defined emotion as "the state of mind that manifests itself by a perceptible change in the body."

It is easy to verify the truth of his words from your own experience. Think back to the last time you became angry? Was it only an emotion, mental anguish? Or did your face flush, your eyes widen, your muscles tighten, your hands tremble?

Think back to a time you experienced fear. Remember the lump in your throat, the knot in your stomach, your racing heartbeat? Have you ever become sick to your stomach because of disgust? Or developed a splitting headache because of tension and worry? None of these symptoms is imaginary. They are caused physically as your muscles tighten or your blood vessels constrict. The result can bring on ulcers or a heart attack.

There are many ways to help you overcome the ailments incurred by anxiety. Doctors suggest that you learn to accept adversity, learn to face challenges with confidence and decision, learn to like people. These all work. But more than anything, you must learn to have confidence in yourself—faith—confidence that all will be well.

Don't accept it on someone else's say-so. Experience its truth and effectiveness in your own life. Shove aside worry and fear and relax. That doesn't mean to say you shouldn't plan for the future. Planning is healthy and constructive. It's the positive approach to living. Worry is unhealthy and destructive. It is the negative approach.

(FK)

~

COUNTING SHEEP

IT'S CALLED INSOMNIA, and it usually takes countless bouts of wearying wakefulness before you recognize that you're suffering from a persistent ailment. In fact, insomnia, the inability to sleep, ranks right behind the cold, stomach disorders, and headaches as the reason thousands of Canadians seek a doctor's help.

Our bedtimes vary according to occupation, social habits, and whether we watch the late news on TV and then get hooked by the late late show. But at least one-third of us—according to a recent Gallup poll—awaken in the middle of the night and are unable to get back to sleep.

Then begins a battle to woo Morpheus: changing position in bed, punching the pillow, wiggling, and squirming. Suddenly you find your mind racing with speculations, problems, doubts, and silly niggling. Now you're fully awake, your brain chasing random thoughts around like a racing greyhound pursuing the mechanical rabbit.

It might go on indefinitely, but you remember your granny's favourite nostrum—count sheep! That may be fine for a shepherd, but "one, two, three . . . ," deadeningly dull though it is, may only succeed in keeping you awake rather than putting you to sleep. There are scores of other snore-inducing favourites: reciting the names of our prime ministers in chronological order, then alphabetically by surname, and then by first name; trying to remember poetry learned in school—anything to focus your mind and prevent it from wandering. Eventually sleep seems several million light-years away.

What do you do about sleeplessness? Time was your doctor might have prescribed a pill or two. But that isn't always the case today. A psychologist, Dr. Michael Stevenson, says sleep is "a natural physiological phenomenon, but it is also a learned behaviour." So how do you "learn" it? Here are some solutions that, individually or in combination, might work for you:

Make sure your bed is comfortable. Get into a position that is relaxed and choose a pillow just thick enough to alleviate shoulder and neck muscle strain.

Use your bedroom only for sleeping—not for such activities as sewing, watching TV, doing office work, or the like.

Mental activity is not conducive to relaxation. Don't take your day's problems or your long-range planning to bed with you. Falling asleep instantly isn't essential. Quiet rest without loss of consciousness is calming, too. Let your mind drift off in pleasant thoughts as you slowly become drowsy.

Eight hours of sleep is not optimum. Some people need less, others more. Determine what works best for you.

If you read in bed, choose something that isn't so exciting or interesting that it wakes you up. And if hunger gnaws, don't waste time battling your growling stomach. Eat something bland to fill the hollow, like bread and fruit, but avoid sugary or heavy snacks.

Avoid stimulants after twilight. Smoking and caffeine-laden liquids, even chocolate, can keep you awake.

Stretching and yawning will help you simmer down. Adopt an "I don't care" attitude; it could help you drift off.

Your general health, digestion, allergies, and even your attitudes play a part in your quest for sleep. If you are an insomniac of long standing, you may not be a subject for self-help. If that's the case you should consult your physician for remedial treatment and possible underlying causes.

You can joke about insomnia just so far. But if you can make one or more of these suggestions work, the sleeping-pill business may find itself dozing off.

(FK)

TAKE *a* WALK

RECOGNITION THAT WE need to improve our health has resulted in enough exercise programs to weary anyone who just thinks about them. Yet the perfect exercise for people of any age is nothing new, startling, or innovative. In fact, it was Hippocrates, the Greek physician who gave medicine its code of ethics 2,060 years ago, who first brought it to mankind's attention . . . walking!

Walking requires less exertion than most sports, yet it provides benefits equal to those gained from most popular workout activities. It remains one of the simplest, yet most effective, of all aerobic exercises—exercises designed to improve respiratory and circulatory functions. In other words, walking is a great strengthener of the lungs and heart. It also aids in reducing cholesterol levels and increasing bone mass.

Officials at Participaction say that several million Canadians of all ages appreciate the joys and fitness benefits of just plain walking.

If you are sceptical about what you can derive from walking, no matter what your age keep this in mind: walking burns off about ninety percent of the calories consumed by jogging. A welcome bonus is that walkers don't develop bad knees or any of the other afflictions common to the running crowd. In addition walkers can usually walk farther than they can run, and they can enjoy themselves more in the course of exercising.

You don't need any special equipment other than a good pair of sturdy, comfortable shoes. You can walk with friends or walk alone. You can follow your own pace, listen to music, or simply enjoy the scenery or the passing parade. And, as a result, you'll

53

get a good night's sleep, reduce accumulated stresses and tensions, and, best of all, shed unwanted pounds.

When you walk, you use up excess calories. How many you expend depends upon how fast a pace you set and how long you walk. If you amble along at a mild three kilometres an hour, for only an hour a day, you will consume 200 calories each time. That's 6,000 calories a month, which adds up to a weight loss of nearly a kilogram a month or about ten kilograms a year. And you need not step out at a faster pace to lose more weight. A program of brisk walking will not add appreciably to the weight loss you can achieve over a similar period of time.

To walk healthfully make sure your shoes are comfortable and give you good support. Walk with your head erect and your tummy tucked in. It is important to use the whole foot; that is, set your heel down first and then roll your foot forward to the toe. If you like to walk briskly, do not take a walk immediately after eating; nor should you walk at a brisk pace when it is very hot or very cold. In extremes of weather a slow steady pace is better than a brisk one. And if you've not been for a long walk in ages, start out with fifteen or twenty minutes and increase that only when you feel ready to lengthen your exercise time.

When beginning a walking program you should start slowly . . . and progress slowly. That means avoiding hills and, at the outset, walking about half a kilometre at the comfortable pace of one hundred steps a minute. In the first week go out only every second day. This will provide your body with a day's rest between each session. Subsequently you can add about another .25 kilometres each week until you can build up to between two and three kilometres with ease and comfort. At that point you can increase your tempo—if that appeals to you—and slowly increase the distance each week. So the next time someone tells you to take a hike, consider it a sensible suggestion.

(FK)

HEALTH PROTECTION
in THE TROPICS

THE REASON YOU go south in the first place is probably to revive yourself in the depths of winter, have a great holiday, and return full of health. So it's worthwhile taking a few precautions to make sure you don't defeat those aims and return in a worse state than when you left.

You may intend to hit the beach and soak up all that nice sunshine, but don't let it get the better of you. Remember your sunscreen (at least a fifteen SPF, higher for children, seniors, and those with sensitive skin), your hat, and your sunglasses or contact lenses with UV protection. Limit your time in the hot sun and wind, particularly at first. For a mild sunburn, apply skin lotion or cream, Caladryl or Calamine lotion, and stay out of the sun. If you get a really bad burn, head for an air-conditioned room, apply cool water or cool baking soda compresses, and take aspirin for one or two days.

Be discriminating about what you eat and drink. Choose exotic food and wine if you wish, but avoid things with a high probability of giving you not just a passing tummy ache or the trots, but possibly a nasty ailment that could accompany you home and stay with you for some time.

Rule number one, doctors advise, is "Don't drink the water," meaning the local water that comes from a tap or in your glass at the table. It's okay to drink bottled water, which you open yourself; beverages such as tea or coffee made with boiling water; canned or bottled soft drinks; beer or wine from a reputable supplier, and, if you can get it, coconut juice directly from the shell (it's good!). Otherwise, even brush your teeth with bottled water or, if necessary, whisky.

Also, swim only in the sea or in pools with chlorinated water; be careful in fresh-water, which may be polluted, and where fresh-water snails may carry a parasitic disease.

Rule number two, which concerns food, is "Cook it, peel it, or leave it." This means, unfortunately, that you should avoid raw vegetables and salads; you eat fresh fruit only if you can wash it and peel it yourself (perhaps take it to your room). Melons are considered unsafe, too. Be sure that all the meat, fish, and shell-fish you eat has been well cooked. This means foregoing dishes like steak tartar, raw or smoked fresh-water fish, and raw clams and other shellfish, which could come from polluted water. You may love such delicacies, but you may not be happy with the consequences.

One more warning. Since hot foods must be hot and cold foods cold, be wary of buffets where the food may be neither.

One of the minor but commonplace hazards of travelling, particularly in warm climates, is diarrhea or Montezuma's revenge. If it hits you, be sure to avoid dehydration by drinking lots of liquids and eating salted crackers. If necessary, try the worldwide remedy for dehydration: half a teaspoon of salt and four teaspoons of sugar to one cup of water. For the symptoms, Pepto-Bismol or Kaopectate may help. If they're bad, seek medical help.

It's wise to check with your doctor well before you leave to make sure you're in good shape to travel, and have any medication you may need to take with you, including, if it's essential you stay on your feet, some remedy for the above-mentioned Montezuma's revenge. Those with drug allergies or other serious conditions may choose to wear a Medic-Alert tag or bracelet.

Make sure your routine immunizations against polio, diphtheria, tetanus, measles, mumps, and rubella are up to date. Depending on where you are going, protection against malaria and other diseases may be required.

(NM)

❦

EATING OUT WELL
& HEALTHY

CHANCES ARE THAT, like most Canadians, you find yourself eating out more and more often, whether it be for business or social reasons or for lack of time to do otherwise. Possibly a third to a half or more of your meals may be eaten in restaurants, hotels, or airplanes. If so, you may wonder if your diet is adequate, or if you are overloading on the wrong things and missing out on what's good for you.

Fortunately, with the current emphasis on a healthy diet, many restaurants are providing really fresh food and offering light alternatives to richer dishes. Mainly it's important to avoid getting too much fat, too much salt, and too many calories, and to favour fresh vegetables and fruit, lean meat, chicken and fish, and whole wheat bread. In restaurants you can do this by choosing carefully and by making your wishes known. "If they aren't listed on the menu, don't hesitate to ask for the ingredients in any dish," advises food scientist Joe Marie Powers, assistant professor in hotel and school administration at the University of Guelph. "Some people may have serious allergies to certain foods like peanuts and peanut oil, or dairy foods, or have other special food needs."

Feel free, also, to ask how foods are prepared; are they broiled, boiled, grilled (preferably), or are they fried? Do they have rich sauces, gravies, or dressings? If so, you can ask that these be served on the side, so you can take a mere dab of them. If the dish is not as you requested (smothered in butter when you asked for none, fried instead of broiled) you have a perfect right to send it back.

Good bets for healthy choices are fish, prepared without

batter (if so, remove it), chicken, meat, baked potatoes without butter or sour cream, fresh vegetables, and salad. And bread or a roll, without butter if you're dieting. Many soups tend to be highly salted, and cream soups high in calories, so consommé or tomato juice are good starters. Limit your drinks, as they only increase your appetite and add calories. And it's better to skip dessert unless it's fresh fruit or cheese.

Sometimes servings are enormous, in which case ask for a smaller portion (or take the surplus home in a doggy bag). Another possibility is to select an appetizer or two and salad and skip the main course entirely.

If you're watching your fat intake and your calories, your choice of restaurant makes a difference. Both Japanese and vegetarian offer plenty of fresh, light food. In others, such as French and Italian restaurants, you'll have to watch your calories and the amount you eat more carefully. Elsewhere you can frequently check out the menu at the door. Fast food restaurants require a certain strategy. There are alternatives to the burger with everything on it, fries and a shake, which can add up to 1,200 calories, as much as a whole day's allowance for a woman watching her weight. You might select instead a plain burger with lettuce and tomato and low-fat milk, for about half the calories. Or you can go for sandwiches without dressing, or a pizza (less salt in it than a hot dog). Coleslaw is a good extra.

More and more restaurants have salad bars. It's good to hit them first, and fill up on greens and such without the dressings, before the main course. If it's cafeteria style, with the desserts displayed in front, choose and eat your main course first; then, only if you must, go back for dessert.

When you are flying, it's possible to order special meals at no extra cost by calling the airline twenty-four hours ahead. You might ask for a vegetarian, low-fat, or low-salt diet, or whatever you require.

(NM)

SICK *of* BEING TIRED?

ARE YOU ALWAYS tired? Have you, in fact, been suffering total fatigue—and for longer than you can remember?

You're not alone. Most, if not all of us, have felt drained, weary, sluggish, exhausted, worn out, or just plain blah at one time or another. And even if a series of symptoms that you can't readily identify is plaguing you, there is probably nothing you can pinpoint to help your family physician determine the cause.

Your ailment usually begins with flu-like problems. You experience a sore throat and some coughing. You probably find that you have a low-grade fever. You may even discover that your glands are swollen.

No, you are not alone; it is estimated that more than 100,000 Canadians are similarly affected. Most are in their twenties or thirties. And for some unexplained reason two-thirds of them are women. So far the cause has proven to be a major mystery. Although the experts have come up with several theories, they can't agree on any one. But they have given it a name: chronic fatigue syndrome or, more popularly, CFS. The daily press has labelled it the "yuppie flu" (though it affects people of all socio-economic groups and of any age). It doesn't help to know it, but the problem is not a new one. It has been recorded under a variety of names and in myriad places for some sixty years at least!

Some physicians doubt that it's a genuine disease. Yet it is all too real to people who are suffering from it. Dr. Richard Earle, co-founder and director of the Canadian Institute of Stress, says that CFS appears to have reached epidemic levels in North America. "Unfortunately," he adds, "no laboratory test has yet been devised to determine the syndrome." The only way it can be diagnosed is by ruling out other possible causes of fatigue such as anemia, thyroid disease, or cancer.

Many researchers put the blame on one virus or another (or even several working together). Others postulate that CFS is caused by a defect in the body's immune system. Psychological factors is the favourite theory of a third group of scientists. Sadly, the debate among the experts tends to overshadow the patients' dilemma. For no matter what its cause, CFS is clearly disabling. Dr. Earle and his associates at the Toronto-based stress centre feel that without laboratory confirmation of an illness, too many physicians refuse to believe that it's real. However, with several decades of solid investigation into various stress-caused debilities, this Canadian research team is convinced that CFS is very real—and that "it is stress related."

It has become clear that prolonged periods of high stress weaken the immune system," says Dr. Earle. The CFS symptoms beyond unrelenting fatigue can include headaches, muscular pain and weakness, the inability to concentrate, and acute distress in family life as well as work life. "Oddly," he adds, "the symptoms may disappear for several years . . . but they often recur."

Stress clearly seems to be the deciding factor in bringing on chronic fatigue syndrome. This is borne out by the most recent studies in Canada and the United States, which show that the majority of CFS patients have high levels of stress and anxiety. And that, at least, seems to dispel the often-heard suggestion that "you're not sick; it's all in your head!"

It provides a hopeful conclusion as well. "If you're a sufferer," says Dr. Dale Matthews of the University of Connecticut Medical School, "you have a treatable disease." It's just a matter of time until researchers come up with a cure.

(FK)

SITTING FIT

TO EXERCISE OR not to exercise? . . . that is not the question. The question is, where do you find the time? It seems as though the major complaint busy Canadians have most often, if they seek to maintain a level of fitness, is the amount of time involved in getting regular exercise.

In some cases, it's more than simply a matter of fitness mainte-nance. There is often the problem of bringing oneself back to a level of acceptable fitness. Getting fit, however, is one thing; there are countless ways in which you can get your muscles back into shape—ways that can be fun as well as healthful.

But staying fit? "Ay, there's the rub," as Shakespeare so aptly wrote. The business day seems too often to stretch beyond eight hours, or even nine hours. People remain confined to their offices, seated behind their desks. They aren't able, in such cir-cumstances, to maintain the muscle tone they so painstakingly built up through a favorite exercise routine. This has become the major frustration for anyone trying to stay in shape.

To counter this problem, Doug MacLennan, senior technical consultant and membership director of the Fitness Institute of Toronto, advises a series of four exercises that you can perform at your desk. This routine, which can be completed in seven or eight minutes, will not only tone sagging muscles and relieve muscle strain, it will also keep you mentally alert, he says.

The Heel and Toe Lift. This is a way to keep your leg muscles in shape, and it is truly a simple one. In fact, not only can it be done while seated at your desk, it can also be practised while strapped into an airplane seat or on a commuter train. Start by leaning forward in your seat, with your hands pressing firmly on your knees. Now lift both your heels off the floor, pressing down with the toes and contracting the calf muscles as tautly as you can. Hold that position for about ten seconds and then lower your heels. Now, with your heels firmly on the floor, raise your toes as high as you can towards your shins—again for about ten seconds. Repeat ten to fifteeen times. This is an exercise you can repeat several times a day.

The Tummy Slimmer. Sit perfectly erect with your spine firmly against your chair-back and your hands gripping your knees. Now exhale, and as you do so, pull in your abdominal muscles as far as you can. Hold that for about five seconds, then relax as you inhale. As you draw in your stomach muscles again, exhale. This should be repeated ten to twenty times and should be done at least once a day. This exercise can also be done on a plane or train without attracting the attention of your fellow travellers.

The Torso Twist. This manoeuvre requires a little space and should probably, therefore, be confined to the privacy of your office or home. Raise your elbows to shoulder level with your hands touching your shoulders. Now slowly twist your torso around to the right as far as you can go. Then reverse the action as far to the left as you can reach. This should be repeated ten to twelve times in each direction.

Head Circles. While this exercise doesn't require any extra room in which to manoeuvre, it may be the kind of movement you'd rather not perform while exposed to the stares of your travelling companions. Nonetheless, in addition to being a great exercise, it's even greater as a muscle relaxer. Keeping your shoulders completely loose, drop your head forward until your chin touches your chest. Now slowly move your head in a large circle five or six times to the left, then reverse direction to move your head in a circle the same number of times to the right.

So even while you sit, there's no excuse for not staying fit.

(FK)

The "SWEET RESTORER"

THE EIGHTEENTH-CENTURY British poet Edward Young, in "Night Thoughts," labelled it succinctly: "Tired nature's sweet restorer, balmy sleep!" In pragmatic modern terms, the quality of the sleep you get makes the quantity of lesser importance. But can you improve the quality of your sleep? And, if so, how?

Medical researchers don't agree on how much sleep is optimum for any one individual. You have to determine that for yourself. However, there seems to be consensus that, on average, seven to eight hours a day will do the trick. In fact, older people appear to require somewhat less sleep than they previously did, though no one has been able to quantify just how much less.

A good way to learn more about your own sleep needs is to keep a diary of your sleep patterns for a couple of weeks. If you feel productive and alert during that test period, the average sleep time you got is probably the amount you need. If not, then experiment to determine your optimum. And once you do so, establish a regular bedtime and wake-up schedule. More important, stick to the schedule even on weekends and holidays.

There is no need to make up for sleep that you lost one night by deliberately getting more sleep the next night. Experiments have shown that sleep deprivation of up to four hours does not affect your performance. In fact, if you get the "normal" amount of sleep the next night, it will compensate for the loss without you having to change your regular sleep pattern.

If you've had a shortfall of sleep the night before, do not try to nap in the middle of the day to make up for the missed rest. This, of course, does not apply if you regularly nap during the day and awaken refreshed, not groggy. A good test for yourself, if you're a catnapper, is whether you dream during your snoozes. If you do dream, it's a sign that mid-day napping more than likely will delay your getting to sleep that evening.

Dr. Charles Pollock, who heads the Sleep-Wake Disorders Center of Montefiore Hospital in New York City, cautions that you should not attempt to reduce the total amount of sleep you've determined necessary for your own best waking-hour performance. Not only will such a plan prove ineffective in increasing your productivity, he says, it can also prove to have a deleterious effect on the body.

One of the most important factors in improving the quality of your sleep is to go to bed relaxed. To accomplish this, avoid exercise within a few hours of your bedtime (other than, per-haps, a brief leisurely walk). And avoid any activities that cause tension—especially arguments.

Try taking a warm bath before bedtime. Read, but not an exciting adventure, or other mind-stimulators, that will keep you turning pages until the dawn breaks. Some people have found that a weak nightcap or snack helps; in fact, many people find milk to be effective. Engage in sex.

Above all, avoid sleeping pills. On a long-term basis they are useless. Some family physicians point out that they can become addictive and potentially dangerous. And if you take them infre-quently, they can produce a drug hangover the next day.

You spend approximately one-third of your life asleep. That's about twenty-three years out of the biblical three score and ten. So make sure the hours you spend asleep are good hours. Shakespeare called sleep "nature's soft nurse." Learn to capital-ize on her tender loving care.

(FK)

SWIMMING *for* HEALTH & PLEASURE

A MIDDLE-AGED executive, who, by dint of sitting at a desk and devouring hearty business lunches, found himself becoming rather portly, decided to take up swimming. Before long he was lapping back and forth for a mile or so every day in a nearby pool.

When travelling he always hit the hotel pool or found his way to the nearest beach or club pool. On holidays he'd explore the length and breadth of bays in the Mediterranean or the Caribbean, navigating on the surface or, with snorkelling equipment, below it.

When visiting a friend's cottage, he'd disappear on the horizon, his wife paddling a canoe protectively behind him, and emerge at the dock an hour later, thrusting out his chest with happiness and good health. Needless to say, his girth declined, and his taste in business lunches now tends towards the lean and green, to keep him fit for what has become his favourite sport.

Then there's the woman who took up swimming to relieve the stiffness in her arm following a mastectomy. Beginning with a length or two of the pool each time, she increased it to a mile a session (about seventy lengths of a large pool), and in the process scored a physical and psychological victory. In good shape again and with renewed confidence, she put behind her all the unpleasantness of her experience.

Swimming is popular for many reasons: for fitness, for social reasons, and for a real sense of well-being. Once you start swimming regularly, it tends to become addictive. Although it rates aerobically right up there with jogging, it's a very relaxing activity, a sort of yoga of the water, guaranteed to banish tension and stress. The hypnotic effect of the regular swimmer's rhythm, stroke, stroke, stroke, stroke, up and down the pool, gives you the aquatic equivalent of a runner's high.

What's attracting many jogging casualties from hard city side-walks, tennis players, and other fitness fans whose knees or feet have given out is the opportunity to get an equal or better physical workout in a medium that spares the weight-bearing joints and stressed ligaments. Termed the perfect exercise, it improves your fitness level in all categories: cardiovascular, flexibility, strength, and endurance.

The nice thing about swimming is that you can work at your own pace, in your own time, improving your strokes or your speed as you go. There are many alternatives to distance or speed swimming. Aquabics, or hydro-aerobics as it's sometimes called, is becoming a popular alternative to aerobic exercises performed on a hard floor. The routine may include warm-up and cool-down stretching exercises at poolside, and water exercises for the legs, arms, and abdominals, emphasizing both flexibility and strength. The resistance of the water to movements adds another dimension. While there are a variety of aquabics classes offered, many keen swimmers simply do a few in-the-water exercises before swimming lengths.

As our Olympic athletes have shown, synchronized swimming is a sport requiring great skill and grace. It can be practised at any level and by all ages, and pays bonuses in streamlining the figure, improving athletic ability, and providing the pleasure of working as a team in an activity that has much in common with dance.

Snorkelling and scuba diving open new worlds for you under-water, as you glide along admiring the strange fish and plant life you see below the surface. Both require the learning of new techniques, and, in the case of scuba diving, lessons are a must. Mastery of swimming comes first, and then, as they say, the world's your oyster.

(NM)

꿍

A LAUGH A DAY

WHEN WAS THE last time you had a good laugh? This morning? Last night? Last week? If you don't remember, you're probably missing out on one of the best ways of keeping your health— even of improving it.

Recent research clearly indicates that laughter is good medicine. Humour makes hospital patients happy, says a nursing coordinator at one of Canada's largest hospitals. And happy patients, she adds, usually promote their own recovery by working harder at it.

When Norman Cousins, the long-time editor of *Saturday Review*, wrote his breakthrough book, *Anatomy of an Illness*, he detailed how laughter had aided his recovery from what had been diagnosed as an apparently incurable degenerative spine disease. His book spurred medical researchers to investigate the role laughter plays in our lives.

A good laugh is more than curative medicine; it is also preventive medicine. But even though adults don't lose their enjoyment of humour, they tend to laugh less and less the older they get. While a four-year-old might laugh as many as 500 times in a day, studies have shown that, on average, an adult manages to laugh only about fifteen times a day!

Just as stress and negative feelings now are known to play a part in impairing your immune system, so positive, laughter-induced emotions are believed to actually boost the immune functions of your body. One psychiatrist who has been studying the physiology of laughter has found that a healthy chuckle actually stimulates the body's internal organs as well as helping to reduce blood pressure and to promote relaxation. In fact, says

Dr. William Fry of the Stanford Medical School, laughter increases the body's immunity to disease.

Other benefits observed to result from hearty belly laughs are improvements in respiration, which, in turn, promote healthy increases of the heart rate and blood circulation.

Laughter is only part of the equation for staying well or for recovering from illness. It has been likened to "inner jogging." One therapist suggests that laughing one hundred times a day is the cardiovascular equivalent of ten minutes of rowing.

So why not try to get more laughs out of your life? First, learn to recognize the amusing side of any situation. Pioneering psychologist William James once wrote, "We don't laugh because we're happy—we're happy because we laugh." Remember those words the next time you're feeling low. Laugh, and see how quickly a black cloud can develop a silver lining.

Laughter has long been a socially acceptable way of purging negative emotions—certainly much more so than rage. Here again, research has come up with an interesting and plausible theory. Annette Goodheart, a West Coast psychotherapist, believes that laughter triggers a massive chemical shift that rebalances the body's stress chemicals.

Being able to laugh at a difficult situation provides the emotional distance you might need to start serious problem-solving. "When you can laugh at a problem," says our family physician, "you're no longer overwhelmed by it."

Remember to laugh with people—not at them. And always be prepared to laugh at yourself. Which leads, inevitably, to the possibility that the next time you phone your doctor with some complaint or other, he'll tell you to take two chuckles . . . and call him in the morning.

(FK)

COUCH POTATOES

TELEVISION VIEWING MAY be hazardous to your waistline.

Those hours spent sitting before the "idiot box" have produced a phenomenon of contemporary society that we have labelled the "couch potato." You recognize the type: a generous waistline and flabby muscles, slouched in a comfortable chair, with one hand dipping into a package of snack food and the other holding the TV remote control.

Research done at Brigham Young University has definitely confirmed the aptness of that depiction. Long hours in front of the home screen go together with obesity, the researchers say, just as "Hockey Night in Canada" goes with a bag of potato chips.

The magazine *Running Times* published some statistics not too long ago that underscore the seriousness of the couch potato syndrome. From their surveys, the jogger's journal extracted the data that thirty percent of women do not participate in any fitness activities whatsoever. And the male members of our society are decidedly worse. The "couch potato jocks" among the "Wide World of Sports" crowd total forty-eight percent.

A cursory glance at those statistics might lead you to conclude that the rest of society—some two-thirds of women and about half the men—participate in fitness activities with some regularity. Wrong! The magazine's survey showed that only twenty-two percent of North American adults keep themselves in shape by working out at least twice a week. The simple act of sitting and watching TV is not only playing havoc with the intellectual capacities of the population, but while we watch we are bombarded with endless commercials mainly for foodstuffs, and most of them in the junk-food category. This encourages the snacking syndrome, with its attendant unneeded calories and a body that grows to look more like a bean bag every day.

To add to the problem, a cyclic relationship develops. The more people sit around, the fatter they get. The fatter they get, the more they want to sit around and the more reluctant they are to exercise. But for couch potatoes the last excuse has just been shot down. The *Journal of the American Medical Association* says that even a minimal amount of exercise will keep you alive longer. How much is a "minimal amount"? The *Journal*'s editors say that a brisk half-hour walk once a day will do the trick.

This miniscule exercise package not only tends to protect you from cardiovascular disease, it can also provide protection against some cancers and a wide range of other problems. Meanwhile, however, if you are addicted to TV, you can get your exercise in front of the tube. There are dozens of exercise videotapes available, and some of them are quite good.

A warning though about those video workout tapes. They have one major flaw: they do not teach you how to exercise properly. Even those videos with narrative voice-overs don't compare correct techniques with incorrect ones. They may tell you what not to do, but they rarely show you what they mean. Without individual monitoring and supervision, beginning exercisers can do themselves serious damage. So before buying an exercise tape for your VCR, take a class with a qualified teacher to learn body awareness and the right alignments. Then you can safely follow a tape, either as a supplemental or primary form of exercise.

Meanwhile, the message is clear. Get off the couch . . . and do it today!

(FK)

THAT AWFUL COLD

THE THING ABOUT a cold is that you either give in to it or you don't. You either soldier on in spite of all, or you succumb to the nasty affliction and give yourself the full treatment, which principally consists of home rest. There are advantages to both approaches.

Some never-say-die characters choose to ignore a cold in spite of non-stop sneezes and sniffles. Since there's no sure cure for it except time, they maintain, you should, as the haughty British medical officer asserted, "treat a cold with the contempt it deserves."

However, depending on your temperament, there are some cures that work wonders. Some women swear on the efficacy of a new outfit, or hat, or blouse, or even a smart scarf. It's a slightly expensive cure, but the lift they get out of choosing something flattering to them seems to banish the cold symptoms immediately. Other people recover miraculously if there's a good party in the offing. I mean, who would miss a party or a big date because of a cold? And it's amazing how the cold symptoms always seem to have disappeared the next day.

If these miracle cures aren't possible, there's much to be said for giving in to the cold completely, staying home and making valiant efforts to cure it. "I reckon being ill is one of the great pleasures of life, providing one is not too ill and not obliged to work till one is better," wrote Samuel Butler in his novel *The Way of All Flesh*, back in the 1800s.

Besides, perhaps the reason you got the cold in the first place was that you were working so hard you were worn out, or the stress was so great you really needed a rest, you tell yourself. So you take a few days off, wrap yourself up in a favourite old dressing-gown, and curl up on the sofa or bed with a good book. If others fuss over you, so much the better.

Once at home, there are several remedies available. An old Scottish remedy for a cold advises you to get into bed, put a bowler hat on each of the two bedposts at the foot of the bed, and drink good Scotch whisky until you see not just two hats but three or more. This remedy may cure your cold, or it may leave you with a hangover and a cold. Another remedy calls for hot lemonade made with fresh lemons, honey, and boiling water. There are those who would add a tot of rum to this brew, although there's no indisputable scientific proof that it's more effective.

Grandmother's favourite remedy of homemade chicken soup has a great deal going for it, and even meets with some medical approval. Since steam does much to clear the nostrils, the steam wafting up from the soup is nicely positioned to do the trick. Besides, if a mother, or mate, or other solicitous soul should serve the soup to you, they provide the necessary TLC a proper cure demands.

Whatever route you go—medicines, chicken soup, hats on the bedposts, or a new outfit—all of these, if you believe in them, may have a placebo effect. A cold often has a psychological component, as the esteemed British Cold Research Unit is the first to admit; they even venture to say that falling in love is a factor. As the old song in *Guys and Dolls* goes, if the guy doesn't do the right thing by her, "a 'poisson' can develop a bad, bad cold." Presumably the course of love can make a cold worse if things are going badly, and better if things are going well. This says much for the powers of love.

(NM)

FARES *of* THE HEART

POLYUNSATURATED FATTY ACIDS. Serum cholesterol and kilo-joules. Aaarh.

Yes, yes, we understand that our diet affects our risk of heart disease. And yes, we know that cardiovascular disease is the number-one killer of Canadians. But please: away with these mind-numbing terms. We don't want to work out a caloric profit-and-loss statement, or determine our cholesterol count in mg/dl. Good grief. One might as well do algebra for fun. We just want to know what to eat and what to avoid. Right? We want an owner's manual for our hearts, written in plain English.

Well, now it's here. The Heart and Stroke Foundation of Canada has produced a straightforward program for people with other things on their minds. *Heart Smart* includes two cookbooks, diet guidelines, a cooking course, and a program for restaurants.

And *Heart Smart* gets right down to basics. Eat a balanced diet that pleases you, but eat less as you grow older. Use less salt, drink less alcohol. And eat less fat—of all kinds. As the *Heart Smart* poster implies, total fat is where it's at.

Maybe—sigh—we do need to know about fats. Saturated fats raise cholesterol levels in the blood, which increases the risk of heart disease. They're found in any animal protein food and higher fat dairy products, in palm and coconut oils, and in hydrogenated vegetable oils. Non-hydrogenated vegetable oils, on the other hand, contain mostly unsaturated fats, which, when consumed in moderation, reduce cholesterol levels or leave them unaltered. Remember, too much fat of any type, either saturated or unsaturated, can cause cholesterol levels to rise.

Knowing this, Canadians are eating more of the lower fat dairy products, salads, cereals, fruits, and vegetables. Good, but we're also shunning red meat, and that's a mistake. Red meat provides protein, B-vitamins, and minerals, particularly iron, and Canadian beef has changed dramatically. Advances in breeding, feeding, and grading systems mean that today's beef is as much as fifty percent leaner and twenty-one percent lower in cholesterol than it was just fifteen years ago. So you're allowed to enjoy that roast or steak. Choose a lean cut, trim away the visible fat, and don't pan-fry it. Broil it, barbecue it, stir-fry it, or roast it on a rack, so the fat can drip away.

To learn more—and to obtain some new and delicious recipes—consult the Heart and Stroke Foundation's best-sellers by Anne Lindsay, *The Lighthearted Cookbook* (Key Porter) and *Lighthearted Everyday Cooking* (Macmillan Canada). And call your local Heart Foundation office—there's one in every province—to find out where and when you can enrol in the ten-hour *Heart Smart* cooking course.

But what about restaurant meals? The Canadian Restaurant and Food Services Association reports that Canadians now eat out five to seven times a week, on average, spending one-third of their food budgets in restaurants. Can we be *Heart Smart* when someone else is preparing the meal?

Yes.

First, look for *Heart Smart* restaurants. The restaurants in most Canadian Holiday Inns now offer *Heart Smart* choices on their menus, as do many independent restaurants. Koya Japan fast-food outlets participate in *Heart Smart*, and some corporate cafeterias also offer *Heart Smart* meals.

In general, we can all be more assertive about food. Consumer demands have already given us new food choices, both at the grocery store and in the restaurant. If we tell grocers and restaurateurs what we want, they'll provide it. A smart heart can still eat hearty. Enjoy.

(SDC)

COPING *with* DEPRESSION

MOST CANADIANS ARE afflicted from time to time with feelings
of depression. They're as common as the head cold, and
shrouded in as many popular misconceptions.

Whether they are short-term and mild, or more serious and
long-lasting, feelings of low self-esteem, aimlessness, and pur-
poselessness are best coped with initially by understanding the
fallacies that exist about being in low spirits.

The most common of these is that the root of any
downhearted feeling is psychological. However, most psychia-
trists insist this is not necessarily so. Medical science has found
that a considerable amount of emotional distress is caused naturally by genetically inherited body chemistry. Nor should you
overlook the fact that many physical illnesses such as viral infec-
tions can cause a depressed state.

Another common belief is that depression does not affect you
physically, only psychologically. The truth is, nonetheless, that
prolonged periods of depression can result in stress and sleeplessness. Stress, as well as lack of sleep, can make you vulnerable
to serious physical problems such as extreme weight loss and,
worse, even multiple sclerosis and heart attack.

Then there are the pill-takers, who firmly believe that tranquilizers help combat feelings of depression. Yet these people
seem to disregard the fact that alcohol and other forms of tranquilizers are all depressants. There are anti-depressant drugs
that can work, but they must be prescribed by your own doctor,
who will do so only after careful consideration of your entire
health situation.

We've even heard it said that people who get depressed

usually don't have strong personalities, that they lack strength of character. Medical science, however, has conclusively proven that, if anything, people with the strongest egos are the most vulnerable to blue moods.

Nor will falling in love lift you out of a depressed state, despite what the writers of popular music and romance fiction would have you believe. In fact, if you are feeling low, you are too internally occupied to be interested in handling a romantic relationship.

Another common notion is that help can only come from long-term psychotherapy. Actually, there are a number of ways in which you can cope with depression. It is important to avoid being isolated, so it is often useful to talk with someone who can listen sympathetically. But if your depression lasts for more than a few weeks, or if your ability to function is impaired, you should seek expert counselling.

It is most important to recognize that your outlook during a low period is going to be pessimistic and distorted. Don't lose sight of that fact when you are depressed. Your judgements of yourself and of your situation as well as of other people are not based on reality. Contemporary thinking holds that depressed moods can be the result of negative feelings about oneself, rather than the cause of them. Recognize, and deny, your self-destructive thoughts and you'll find yourself in an "up" mood. In fact, you can overcome depression by rooting out your belief that the world is bleak and that you are worthless.

And while it may be difficult, try to keep active. Do things, and see people. Don't fall for the misconception that there are usually after-effects from depression. In fact, it is often possible, after a bout of melancholy, to jump right back where you were with no residual effects.

So fight back. You'll recover more quickly.

(FK)

III

KNOWING

THYSELF

❧

The TIME *of* OUR LIVES

HISTORIAN WILL DURANT once remarked that no man who is in a hurry is quite civilized. By Durant's standards, we have all become barbarians—heads down, jaws clenched, charging grimly through our lives.

Don't talk to us: we don't have time. Since scarcity creates value, time has become our most valued commodity. In the 1990s, it seems, the true measure of wealth is not discretionary income, but discretionary time.

We hoard, guard, and manage our time with the intensity of a pension-fund manager reviewing the portfolio.

Research confirms what instinct tells us: North Americans have more money than ever, and less freedom. Recent surveys show that leisure time has dropped by thirty-two percent since 1973, while the work week has expanded from forty-one to forty-nine hours. In two-income families seventy-three percent of the women say they have too little leisure and so do fifty-one percent of the men. Today's professionals routinely work sixty and eighty hours a week, and their paper-burden has increased by 600 percent in twenty years.

We were expecting just the opposite. In the mid-1960s, social scientists forecast a twenty-two-hour work-week by the 1980s. Clever robots and intelligent appliances would bring us the cashless marketplace, the paperless office, and freedom from household drudgery. The big social problem would be "education for leisure."

Instead, we confronted inflation, deregulation, and global competition. New desires became needs, and prices outpaced incomes. Today's car has air-conditioning, heated seats, and power-everything and it costs what a house once cost. Expectations, too, have risen much faster than incomes. Why shouldn't everyone have winter vacations, second cars, summer cottages, satellite dishes, VCRs, home computers, cellular phones? Don't our kids have a right to ski trips and fencing lessons, magnificent stereos and perfect teeth?

We want it all. To pay for it all, we work overtime, sink into debt, and worry continuously.

What we've lost, says Halifax psychologist Dr. Bradley McRae, is "uncontaminated leisure," otherwise known as "quality time." That's the time we spend on things we value just for themselves—hanging around with our children, visiting friends, pursuing hobbies, travelling, reading, reflecting.

In *Practical Time Management*, McRae describes the highest quality time as "flow experiences," moments in which a person is utterly immersed in an experience, losing all sense of time and self. "In the 1980s we concentrated so much on efficiency that we actually tried to schedule our quality time," says McRae. "But it just doesn't work that way."

Quality time does not appear on demand—and the quality of our time is related to its quantity. The parent who shares flow experiences with a child invariably spends a lot of time with the child—not just a scheduled hour or two, but lazy Saturdays and unhurried evenings. Like happiness or love, flow experiences blossom at unpredictable moments, but only in fertile conditions. We know enough now to demand quality goods. Our new demand for quality time will reshape career choices, labour relations, education, and retail business. It may even lead us back to such apostles of simplicity as Henry David Thoreau, whose only time-saving equipment was a sane mind and a cheerful outlook.

"Time," said Thoreau, "is but the stream I go a-fishing in."

(SDC)

SHED *a* TEAR

WHEN WAYNE GRETZKY shed some tears the day he announced his departure from Edmonton for the warmer climes of Los Angeles, the press and TV lapped it up. The Great One's feelings overflowed through his eyes, and the world was made privy to that moment on front pages and in the evening newscasts.

Other athletes have shed tears in public. Some with more provocation, others with less. And athletes aren't the only ones known to cry in-voluntarily as an expression of emotion. Shortly after the end of World War II in Europe, a Canadian colonel was driving through Germany. He passed lines of ragged, tired German soldiers just released from prison camps, now trudging hundreds of miles back to their homes and families.

"Strange," the officer said later, "last week I hated their guts. Now I suddenly saw them as human beings hurrying back home to become husbands, to rear children, and to till the soil. Before I realized it, I found that I was crying." The point to be considered is that our culture has taught us—perhaps for thousands of years—that it is unmanly to cry. Only women weep, our mothers told us. Men—especially strong men—suffer in silence. Shakespeare's tragic hero King Lear experiences the greatest heartbreak of his life when he is dispossessed by his two daughters. But will he weep? He will not. He says: "Let not women's weapons, water-drops, stain my man's cheeks!"

In other cultures it is quite permissible for a man to shed tears in public. Among the Innu, men weep without losing status in the eyes of the community. The Maori of New Zealand accept that warriors will weep. It is not uncommon in Latin countries to see men shed tears in public. Are the French, Spanish, and

Italians simply more emotional by nature? Or is there a possibility that their men realize the value of a good cry now and then?

Scientists have been telling us for the past decade or more that crying may actually be good for us on occasion. A distinguished American epidemiologist, Dr. James Bond, has said that modern man might add years to his life if he would break down and weep once in a while. "Or," he added as a sop to our mothers' teachings, "if he could find a male equivalent for tears."

Tears aren't always triggered by sorrow, sympathy, grief, or a train of thought. Sometimes sheer beauty is enough to bring on an outburst. Actor Charles Laughton, spotting a bank of massed daffodils and narcissuses on a university campus, is reported to have burst into tears at the movingly beautiful sight. History records famous men who wept in public. Alexander the Great wept because there were no more worlds left for him to conquer. (Will Donald Trump react the same way someday?) Scipio spoke of "the gracious gift of tears." Lincoln was proud of his ability to weep for relief and in sympathy. And what Bible reader does not know that Jesus wept.

So the next time you feel close to tears, let them come. You'll be better off for it. After all, why try to be tough with a mixed-up inside when it's just as easy to be a little less tough with a well-adjusted inside.

You know what happens when you tie down the safety valve on a steam engine. So don't tie down the safety valve on your emotions. You may actually be helping yourself live a longer, happier, and better-adjusted life.

(FK)

TEMPER! TEMPER!

"THREE MINUTES OF anger will sap your strength quicker than eight hours of work."

That statement by a noted family counsellor, the Reverend Charles W. Shedd, sharply spotlights how devastating a temper can be. It clearly asks the question: can you afford your temper? Temper, said Dr. Shedd, can be the most expensive thing in your life. Too many unhappy marriages result from the uncontrolled temper of a marriage partner. Dr. Shedd told of a man who didn't like the dinner his wife cooked and threw it at her. A woman who raged because her husband spent too much on clothing ripped up everything in his closet.

Childish! Unreasoning! Temper usually is. And even when it is justified, it's costly to the person who indulges in it. Dr. Walter Alvarez, a widely read newspaper columnist and staff physician at the Mayo Clinic, said that temper puts a terrific strain on your body. "When you are angry, your blood rushes to the major muscles of your arms and legs. Thus you have greater physical strength, but your brain, lacking its full blood supply, is cut down in efficiency. That is why when you are angry you say things you do not mean and do things that seem outlandish." The picture of a typical marital spat.

Bad-tempered people apologize for their actions to those they offend. They try to make up for things they say and do. And, often, their friends or marital partners will forgive them. But temper has broken many a marriage and even more friendships. Worse, the angry ones can't forgive themselves. Each letting-go takes something from them. It diminishes them in addition to being costly to their health.

Doctors know that many of the body's ills come from attitudes of anger, hate, and resentment. Dr. Alvarez wrote that many a sick man or woman has recovered by the simple process of substituting patience for impatience, calmness for anger, and love for hate. The once-suggested "blow off steam" theory is rarely if ever encouraged today. Such a temporary release lacks the curative power of replacing hate with love.

Thousands know the terrible cost of temper to peace of mind. Anger costs the cooperation and good opinions of others, their affection and regard. It is, in effect, a disease. It needs to be faced and cured, lest it rob us of beauty and dignity.

If you and your spouse are prone to losing your tempers with each other, why not develop a set of combat regulations—your own sort of Marquess of Queensberry rules. It is essential that married couples abide by one overriding dictum when tempers break out at home: fight fair! For example, don't criticize things that probably can't be changed. A spouse's limited earning power is not a fair target. On the other hand, it's dangerous to stew in silence if your partner leaves dirty clothes on the floor, or chews with mouth agape. Minor irritations fester.

Don't leave the house during a fight. You'll be talking to yourself—your own best supporter. The result is that you'll get a self-serving reconstruction of what happened rather than an objective new view of the situation.

If you're getting nowhere after a long stretch of quarrelling, simply stop. Don't say a word. Your spouse will have great difficulty arguing solo. You can always resume the next day. And don't sulk after the real fighting is over. Pride has no place here. The winner of the fight should be the one to initiate the reconciliation.

Self-analysis helps. If temper fits follow a pattern, they can be forestalled. Anger may come with fatigue, a let-down, or with worry; and half the battle is won if such tendencies are recognized. The price of temper is so high, no one can afford it.

(FK)

READING PEOPLE

WE MAKE CONTACT with scores, sometimes hundreds, of people during the course of our business and personal lives. Some we know well, some hardly at all. These daily relationships depend on our ability to communicate effectively. But because communication is a two-way street—reaching out to people while receiving information from them—we sometimes fail in our efforts.

How often, for example, have you conducted business with individuals whose words didn't seem to add up meaningfully? Or physical demeanour? How many times have you met someone socially and felt that the words spoken were empty because they were accompanied by eyes that seemed to say nothing. These poker-faced people have emotions. They react to the world around them, but their expressions betray nothing about their thoughts unless you learn to read their faces as well as their words.

First, you must be able to keep a stalled conversation flowing. The key is to steer the dialogue towards feelings and emotions rather than details. Avoid such common colloquial mistakes as bombarding your companion with questions, being quick to offer advice, or disclosing too many personal details.

Probably the most vital factor in good communications is the ability to listen, a discipline that should be made mandatory in school curriculums. To listen effectively you must relax. That will enable your conversational partner to relax as well. The result is smoother communication between you. Pay full attention to what is being said, and maintain eye contact. Don't be put off by your partner's tone of voice or manner; nervousness or misplaced emotions can cloud the speaker's message. Listen closely to points you disagree with—a poor listener will shut these out or distort them, diminishing comprehension almost totally.

Avoid having your mind wander when the speaker pauses. Your brain can race ahead four times faster than normal conversation, and you'll soon lose your train of thought—and your interest. Above all, don't decide on the basis of someone's mannerisms or outward appearance that they have nothing interesting to say.

And what about those unspoken thoughts behind a poker face? Watching people's actions can bring you a lot closer to the truth than merely listening to words. For example, if the speaker fidgets a great deal, clears his throat, jiggles a key chain, tugs at an ear, or wrings his hands, you know he's nervous.

What other body language will unlock the innermost thoughts of your companion? Are his arms crossed, or his speech punctuated with karate-like chops and finger-pointing? Those mannerisms, says Dr. Martin Groder, a psychiatrist and business consultant, indicate the speaker is defensive about his position. Does he rub his eyes or nose, glance sideways away from direct eye contact? He's showing suspicion about what you're saying.

An open person will not clench her fists. Her jacket will not be buttoned. If she sits on the edge of her chair with upper body leaning forward, you'll find her cooperative. If she strokes her chin, keeps a hand on her face, touches hand to nose, or peers over her glasses, she's evaluating your conversation seriously. But if she's slumped in her chair and fails to make eye contact, she's nervous and unhappy with the situation. The man who steeples his hands, keeps them behind his back, in his jacket pockets with thumbs out, or grasping his coat lapels, is full of confidence.

So be wary: choose your own words carefully, and remember that your face and body can give away your inner feelings.

(FK)

The BIG FIVE-O

A WRITER WE know sailed by his fiftieth birthday with nary a whimper—until some four months after the fact. Then he sank into what our Victorian forebearers used to call "a blue funk." What brought it on was seeing the "About the Author" blurb attached to an article he had written for a major Canadian periodical. It described him as "a fifty-year-old author and journalist." Reading the "fateful news in black on white," as he put it, triggered the realization that his life had reached a benchmark.

There is no doubt that the fifty-year plateau brings with it change for some people. Those who aspired to reaching positions of influence in their professions have probably already done so. Offspring are grown up; there may a grandchild or two on the scene, or at least on the horizon. And there is a chance that one or both of your parents are dead. That last factor sometimes creates a sense of panic: are you now the "older generation"?

There are some who, having enjoyed the existence of five decades, suddenly look back and fear that their dreams of life achievements, or the achievements themselves, may have to be given up. The so-called mid-life crisis (whenever that's supposed to be reached, and whatever it turns out to be) has been sparked by an unwarranted awareness of mortality, possibly by some outside event that involves a loss of one kind or another.

But there should be no fears, no crisis—imagined or otherwise. Mid-life is the time to find a sense of balance within yourself. It is a time to take comfort in accepting yourself regardless of your achievements. Most important, it is a time to reassess, a time to set new and perhaps more appropriate goals for the years to come.

How do you do this?

Recognize that the years past and the years to come must each be appreciated for what they are. There are some goals that did not perhaps become reality as rapidly as you once expected. There are goals that were not quite realistic. But you are now able to enjoy your leisure time much more, to enjoy things that exist for the moment, at the moment. And with this realization, you should be able to ease off on the pressure to reach goals. Flexibility in your thinking and your lifestyle is the goal you have achieved, whether or not you planned for it consciously; henceforth it is going to make life more pleasurable.

You can now bend away from disciplinary attitudes that, in years past, you may have taken from time to time. You can take comfort in the fact that, having earned the respect of those around you, you can abandon authoritarian stances you may have taken towards others.

Now is the time to recognize the values of friendships, if you haven't already done so. Now is the time you can look to renewing those associations that earlier pressures of business and family may perhaps have forced you to let slip. Acceptance of oneself often generates a recognition of dependency on other humans. So this can become a time of intensifying friendships, or appreciating human relationships and, especially, of reinforcing your relationship with your spouse.

This is the time for a spiritual awakening, the time to see yourself as an important link in the chain between past and future generations. You may find a common energy shift from social and political activities to more spiritual and aesthetic concerns.

It all comes down to an appreciation of life's basics. Status symbols seem to lose their importance. Good health becomes something for which you are thankful. So, welcome to the big five-O!

(FK)

DISABILITIES— THEIRS & OURS

TO MOST, THE term "disability" means wheelchairs, white canes, hearing aids, the spasms of muscular dystrophy, and the physical deformities from Thalidomide. We shudder and sympathize. We thank our lucky stars that we were spared. These are visible disabilities. Invisible disabilities we tend to ignore, although they are just as serious.

A disability is what makes *them* the disabled, different from *us* who are "normal." Normal means that comfortable majority of us who are white, Anglophone or Francophone, Protestant or Catholic. The rest, the Native peoples, Asians, Blacks, and Hispanics, we call "visible minorities" and by so doing place them at an immediate disadvantage, conferring on them a gratuitous disability.

The irony of this attitude is that in one way or another we are all disabled and spend the bulk of our lives fighting to overcome handicaps with which we have been saddled. Migraine headaches, angina, vertigo, even the two hours spent driving to and from work each day impose a disadvantage relative to those who live only a short walk from the job. An unemployed Toronto factory worker has a decided advantage over an unemployed fisherman living in Burgeo, Newfoundland, where fishing is the only work in town. During a drought year, a prairie wheat farmer suffers the same sort of disability. We judge disabilities only by what we see and hear. There is no way to suppress a persistent stutter, hide a club foot, or disguise Down's syndrome. Neither can we change the colour of our skin nor master the English or French language in the vernacular unless we learned it at our mother's knee. Although all levels of government and

89

business profess equality in their social, educational, and hiring practices, trumpeting support for our multi-cultural, multi-racial society, the fact remains that some men and women, many with enormous talents, are excluded from opportunities they deserve.

The immediate result of excluding minorities, of whatever description, from society's mainstream is that we force into ghettos those very people upon whom our future survival as a nation depends. With a birth rate hovering around 1.6 per couple, our existing self-satisfied majority will be extinct within five generations, according to Statistics Canada. Officially, we welcome diversity, but we are slow to accept what others can contribute to our society.

We will accept disabilities if they are invisible. An observer cannot see a migraine headache, or hear deafness, or feel a cancerous tumor growing next to a shaky heart. Yet, if violinist Yit hak Perlman or physicist Stephen Hawking struggled into a Canadian government or corporate personnel office for a job interview, would either of them be hired? Hungarian born George Faludy, the distinguished writer and poet who became a Canadian citizen in 1976, observed that it was the physically weak but mentally alert, not the physically strong dullards, who survived the labour camp in which he was imprisoned. "Without exception all those who lectured, and all those who learned to listen, survived."

We must all learn to listen and see, not our collective disabilities, which are many, but the unique creativity and generosity of understanding that lie within each of us to make this country a better place for everyone.

(TF)

OUTSIDE INTERESTS

DURING THE EARLY part of this century railway work was considered to be among the ten best occupations in Canada, on a par with doctors, lawyers, and stockbrokers. Yet the results of a survey made during the early 1930s by Canadian National Railways showed that most of its employees were dead three years after they retired. In a footnote the report observed that "the few employees who continued to lead active lives after retirement survived well into their seventies and early eighties."

After the mandatory staff party, formal presentation of a gold pocket watch or pen and pencil set, followed by monthly pension cheques, the employer considered its obligations to each employee fulfilled. They parted company on the best of terms. But for those who experienced such brief enjoyment of their sunset years it seems hardly fair.

Is there a solution? The answer lies, as the CNR report observed, in leading "active lives after retirement." In other words, developing outside interests. In short, a hobby.

Whether we work a forty- or seventy-hour work-week each of us needs a diversionary interest to take us away from the stress and responsibilities of our occupation. By shifting our attentions to an alternative interest, we force occupational stress into the subconscious part of our minds while the active part of our brain engages in something different. Every outside interest or hobby is, as Dr. David Saltzman describes, "a therapy of alternatives" for the busy worker in helping to relax and cope with long-term stress. These alternatives or "hobbies" can be a strenuous sports activity, starting up a new business enterprise, or the sedentary enjoyment of a good book. Whatever the choice, stress is offloaded by concentrating on something fresh that provides personal interest and appeal.

Today's society is very different from the one described in the CNR report. Through advances in medicine, diet, and regular exercise our life span has been extended. So, too, have our years of productive energy. Members of the Canadian Forces routinely retire at age forty-five on full pension. Many airline pilots are grounded at age sixty with handsome pensions. Most corporate and government executives or employees receive the golden handshake at age sixty-five. In nearly every case, these retirees face another ten to twenty-five years of active and productive life.

If they have been wise enough to develop alternative interests for their talents and energies, then their later years should be filled with pleasure and an enormous sense of accomplishment. Prime Minister Winston Churchill became a bricklayer and artist. In his seventies and eighties, no longer able to carry bricks, he continued to paint. United States President Franklin Roosevelt collected stamps. When her marriage fell apart, Agatha Christie turned her hobby of writing and travelling into a prolific career of producing popular mystery stories. She, too, died in her eighties.

Whether you try your hand at a new business venture, laying bricks, or raising a forest of bonsai trees, the important thing is to direct your attention away from the stress of your vocation at regular intervals and to spend time on something that may, ultimately, turn out to be far more important to your happiness and longevity than you realize. And, it's never too late to start.

(TF)

YOU TOO CAN
BE CREATIVE

YOU DON'T HAVE to wear a beret and sport a long paintbrush to be creative. You don't have to be an artist, writer, musician, filmmaker, or designer. In fact, with a little practice, anyone can be creative in his or her own way.

A dash of creativity helps in all fields, from cooking, teaching, science, or the arts to the nitty-gritty of the business world. Essentially, it means a new way of looking at things so that fresh concepts can emerge. This can be enormously helpful in working out a business plan, as well as in selling and advertising, and even in the details of productions. Isn't there a better way that each procedure can be accomplished?

There used to be some mistaken ideas about creativity. A creative person was thought to be slightly mad. Then there was the mystical idea that inspiration came to the creative person out of the blue, like a flash of illumination. More recently, creativity has been connected with a high IQ, a theory that has since been disproven. Although some people are obviously more creative than others, partly through habits of thinking developed since childhood, anybody can learn to be creative to some degree. You don't create ideas out of the blue; you must have something to create them from. What you do to create is combine your ideas and impressions in a unique fashion to come up with something new. You churn around your past experience and emotions to reveal new and unexpected insights. The process, according to psychologists, involves a partnership with the subconscious. You mull over the problem in your mind, then "sleep on it," literally or for a period of time. Then come back to it for a fresh, and possibly inspired, look. The open mind, which is receptive to fresh ideas and sensory impressions, is more apt to be creative. It helps to suspend judgement and belief for a time, in order to accept new ideas, no matter how crazy they may appear at first. Let the ideas come, throw them out to the group, get them down on paper in a rough draft, do a quick sketch before looking at them again with a critical eye.

It helps if your creativity can be focused, concentrated on one objective. You're thinking about how to build a better mouse-trap, or a new sales pitch for the mousetrap, rather than just waiting for a bright idea of any kind to occur.

Although the natural creativity of children is often squelched by teaching that emphasizes memorization, acceptance of the statement of authorities, or the need to always give "the right answer," it can be encouraged by sensitive teachers, even reacti-vated in later years.

If the work environment is stimulating, if the group is com-posed of people of different backgrounds, new ideas are more likely to proliferate. Managers who are sympathetic to new ideas rather than rigid in their thinking are more apt to encourage originality in members of their staff.

One method of stimulating new ideas is brainstorming. Mem-bers of a group sit around for twenty minutes to an hour airing ideas off the top of their heads as solutions to a problem. It's a mutual stream-of-consciousness, one-idea-leads-to-another sort of session. People must be reassured that their ideas may be far out; practical aspects will be considered later. It works best if there's a leader of the discussion who keeps things on track, who encourages people to contribute rather than shooting down crazy ideas. The leader should be non-committal, saying things like "That's interesting. Any other suggestions?"

It's surprising how creative people can become in a lively group, and individually, too, if they just stop to look around themselves in a new way.

(NM)

OLD DOGS, NEW TRICKS

IN 1933, PRESIDENT Franklin Delano Roosevelt paid a call on Mr. Justice Oliver Wendell Holmes. He found Holmes sitting on his verandah, reading Plato in the original Greek.

"Why do you read Plato, Mr. Justice?" he asked.

"To improve my mind, Mr. President," said Holmes. He had been retired from the U.S. Supreme Court for just two years— and he was ninety-two.

There is a wicked falsehood abroad in our land: the notion that aging somehow withers our minds and destroys our ability to learn. We almost seem proud of our refusal to grow old. You can't teach an old dog new tricks, we say. I'm too old to learn Spanish, or bookkeeping, or navigation. Retraining? Ha! I've worked in this factory all my life, and I'm too old to be trained for anything else.

Yet continuous learning is the key to our future. Forecasters predict that today's young workers will upgrade, change jobs, or even switch careers four or five times in their working lives. North American corporations spend more than $60 billion a year on training. One Canadian in four is not fully literate, and whole towns may have to retrain themselves. We *must* teach our old dogs new tricks—and old dogs *can* learn them. The real issue is attitude.

"From laboratory studies we have good evidence that people can learn at any age," says Dr. Fergus Craig, head of the University of Toronto psychology department. "With older people it takes longer because the nervous system is less plastic, less flexible, and it make changes less easily." Studies at the University of Waterloo, for instance, show that older people don't remember recently learned skills in chess or bridge as well as younger people.

But, says Craig, it's also a well-established fact that learning is related to your expertise in a particular area. If you know a lot about Russian history, you'll absorb new information about Ivan the Terrible much more quickly than someone who knows nothing about Russia—no matter how old you are.

In practical terms, adult educators agree that the key factor is not innate ability, but attitude. Dean Douglas Myers of Dalhousie University's Henson College notes that the actual capacity to learn is much less important than maximizing that capacity—at any stage in life. Your capacity is always "far greater than you use and far greater than you thought."

Older students attend university not from inertia or family tradition, but from economic need or passionate desire. Their attitude and commitment makes them a joy to teach, says Myers's colleague Dr. Stephen Frick. "They have higher standards than young students," Frick says. "They're very hard on themselves; they feel they've let everybody down if they get Bs." Older students do well in the humanities and social sciences, where they must synthesize information and find patterns in it. Their experience helps them see the patterns.

"History, for example, is kind of lost on people who are eighteen," Frick says. "To someone of forty, history makes sense."

The best news of all is that "learning to learn" is itself a form of expertise. Some lucky people—like Mr. Justice Holmes—love knowledge for its own sake, and never stop learning. Such people develop important skills and habits: paying attention, separating the important material from the background, developing shortcuts and aids to memory. "There's an element of use-it-or-lose-it, the same as with your body," says Needa Chappell, Director of the University of Manitoba's Centre of Aging. Keep your mind active, and it'll be fine in old age. "You can't teach an old dog new tricks," someone once said to an undergraduate in her sixties.

"True," she replied. "I'm glad I'm not a dog."

(SDC)

PROMISES, PROMISES

"Never promise more than you can perform," said Publius Syrus, around 42 B.C. Good advice, then and now. Why do we still ignore it?

Nothing is more infuriating than a broken promise, the consequences of which range from annoyance to tragedy. Behind the divorce, the failing grade, the cancelled order is usually a string of broken promises. We mean well, but we promise too easily and thoughtlessly, and our casual promises are simply forgotten.

Broken promises destroy trust, and trust is the foundation of our lives together. In our businesses, our families, our pastimes, we rely on trust every day. Without trust, we could neither plan nor predict. We trust that the report will be printed, that our spouse will be home by 5:30, that our employers will pay us on time. We plan our business meeting, our anniversary dinner, and our mortgage payment on the basis of that trust. And trust is based on just one thing: a long chain of promises—expressed or implied—have been met.

"If you want me to trust you," says Vancouver consultant Neil Godin, "just do the things you say you are going to do . . . again and again."

Godin's consulting specialties are human resource development and business turnarounds. His team-building program has been used at every level from the executive suite to the shop floor. Its first step is the creation of a "Team Code of Commitment" by the embryonic team itself. Every Team Code begins with a pair of items on which Godin will not compromise; they are pre-printed on the form he uses.

The first item in the Team Code says that team members will not "make 'casual' [casually considered] commitments to each other." The second item says that when team members do make a commitment, they are giving their word; they can be trusted to keep their promise.

Godin's objective is to create smoothly functioning teams that meet, brainstorm, develop, and implement action plans. The supervisor becomes a facilitator and monitor rather than a boss, and the unit becomes self-managing. But the whole process fails without a shared commitment to honour promises. "If the team won't accept those basic commitments," Godin says, "the project can't possibly work and should be abandoned."

What techniques can help us keep our promises?

• Learning to say No. In our eagerness to please, we promise more than we can achieve. When someone asks the impossible, tell them it's impossible and suggest alternatives. If it's a silly idea, delay any action and let it die.

• Realism. "If asked when you can deliver something, ask for time to think," says Robert Townsend in *Up the Organization*. "Build in a margin of safety. Name a date. Then deliver it earlier than you promised."

• Deadlines. Don't say you'll do it "As soon as I get a chance." Say when you'll do it—at least to yourself—or admit up front that you probably won't ever get around to it. Ask others for firm deadlines, too.

• Written Records. Promises can't slip your mind if you write them down in your planning calendar or pocket diary. If someone makes a promise to you, note that, too—and suggest that he or she also make a note of it. Your note shows that you really do expect the promise to be kept, and implies that you'll check up later on.

• Follow-up. Every day, scan your calendar to see what commitments are coming up, and what preparations need to be made.

Help your colleagues to keep their promises by checking with them a few days in advance, just to be sure they remember.

These tips will help—and that's a promise.

(SDC)

DID YOU FORGET?

DO YOU TEND to forget appointments or anniversaries? Do you misplace your car keys, eyeglasses, or gloves more often than you care to admit? Do you sometimes forget to follow through on tasks you promised to take care of? If you answered yes to any of the above, don't feel bad. You're like most of us, hurried, harried, and hopelessly trying to keep track of dozens of bits of unrelated information every day. It's not that you have a poor memory—you simply have an untrained one.

People have two kinds of memory: short-term and long-term. The former is the kind you use to recall things you may need within the next few hours or days. The latter is used to store away information you will need in weeks or months to come. With short-term memory, most people seem to be able to remember a half-dozen or so items. With long-term memory, there seems to be no limit to how much you can absorb.

Interestingly, information is automatically passed from the "short-term memory file" to the "long-term memory bank." For example, consider the phone number your colleague told you about yesterday. When you call it today, you'll look it up. And the same tomorrow. But by the third or fourth time you have to make that call, chances are you'll do so without a second thought. The transfer from the file to the bank will have taken place without conscious effort on your part.

Sometimes you're put into the position of having too many new bits of information to file away at one time. So how do you go about improving your memory? Here are four simple steps you can take to help overcome the problem:

• Write things down. Whenever you get a piece of information that you must remember, record it in writing. Transferring data to written form is one of the best ways to overcome memory loss.

• Repeat the message. Like committing it to writing, repetition is very helpful in implanting the information in your mind.

• Try to form a mental picture. If you're introduced to several people at once, for example, look for associations to help with their names. Mr. White may have white hair. Mr. Beaudoin may be wearing a bow-tie. And Mr. Diamond could be wearing a jewelled ring. Sound silly? Yes, but it's effective; soon you won't even think of the associations you made the first time you met them.

• Ask for help. Don't be ashamed to admit that you're being overwhelmed with information. Ask to be reminded if you haven't responded to a request.

One of the main reasons you tend to forget is that you sometimes don't listen as well as you should. Obviously, if you haven't heard something you can hardly be expected to remember it. So sharpen your listening skills. Listen attentively when people are talking to you; give them your undivided attention. If you allow distractions to interfere you can't receive the information you need.

Always repeat things for clarification. If you've had a request made of you, or have been given some new information, repeat it immediately. That way, both you and the person with whom you are communicating will be sure the message has been understood. Finally, be careful not to allow any prejudice to interfere with what you're listening to. It's quite common to pay more attention to some people than to others. Conversely, less credence is often given to what is said by some people. If you assume information is not important, you are less likely to remember it later.

And above all, don't be upset if you do forget sometimes. Everyone does.

(FK)

SPIRIT *of* IMAGINATION

IN 1895, WHEN he was sixteen years old, Albert Einstein was moved to wonder what a man might see if he were sitting on the tip of an advancing beam of light. The question was one of the speculations about the nature of light and movement, time, and space, that allowed Einstein to up-end physics ten years later, giving us a fresh new vision of the nature of nature.

Einstein's "thought experiment" illustrates the colossal power of the imagination, one of the most vital and least understood powers of the human mind.

Imagination underlies all the sciences, all our great enterprises, and most of daily life. It is not just the province of artists and other unusually "creative" people. How could we apply for a job, enter a marriage, raise a child, or buy a house without imagining and desiring the results of these actions?

The story of Canadian business is a long record of entrepreneurs putting their money where their imagination was: Samuel Cunard imagining steamships making punctual trans-Atlantic crossings; Roy Thomson, with $200 in his pocket, imagining himself a newspaper owner in Timmins; the Reichmann brothers shrewdly foreseeing that New York would overcome its financial crisis. Every business in Canada first took shape in someone's reveries.

"Action begins with fantasy," said the innovative educator John Holt. "We are very unlikely to do something new, difficult, and demanding until after we have spent some time imagining or dreaming of ourselves doing it." For the poet Coleridge, the imagination was "the living power and prime agent of all human perception," the faculty that determines what we actually see and notice. Yet our culture remains wary of imagination. Most children have vivid imaginations; most adults have learned to suppress them. The imagination is uncontrollable; it reveals awkward truths and shatters our conventional view of things. It is thoroughly unpredictable. We may be hoping for a missing rhyme or a brilliant business idea, but the imagination is just as likely to deliver exotic inventions, practical jokes, or erotic fantasies.

We are appalled to find such thoughts in our minds; those vagrant notions belong not to reputable citizens like ourselves, but to fringe characters. We expel the ideas, and sigh with relief.

The problem, of course, is that a horde of other ideas also depart—including the ones we wanted. Our unruly notions wait till our mental barricades have been lowered by alcohol, fatigue, or sleep. Then we plunge into bizarre trips in warped and distorted time sequences, scenes of ecstasy and terror, rollicking adventures, thrilling games, and Technicolor improprieties.

Dreams are our most accessible route to the subconscious, which is to the imagination as the stream-bed is to the stream. Our sleeping minds, free-wheeling through the velvet night, make a kaleidoscope from the fragmented concerns of our daylight minds, turning them over and changing their shapes, fitting them together in strange ways, and presenting us, in the morning, with a complete and finished solution to yesterday's problem. No wonder we want to "sleep on the deal"; our dreaming minds exercise powers we had forgotten we possessed.

Even a neglected imagination persists, dormant, waiting to be respected and recognized. To exercise it, we need only to trust it, and to find in ourselves enough courage to heed its promptings. We will be generously rewarded. Without imagination, there can be no vision. And without vision, all our ventures come to naught.

(SDC)

❦

VOICING SUCCESS

IF YOU'RE AT all like the rest of us, you probably think more about how you look than how you sound. After all, your appearance can help ease your way up the ladder of success. But your speech patterns are part of your appearance, too, and they can be powerful in helping you gain success.

Consider this: about forty percent of the initial impression you project to others is based on the sound of your voice. Only about ten percent comes from what you actually say. Is it any wonder, then, that a strong, confident voice can boost your effect on the job.

In making any sort of business presentation—a speech to stockholders, a sales pitch, or a proposal to your boss—if your voice is weak or drones on, you may be sabotaging a great idea . . . and yourself.

How might your voice be holding you back? Its pitch can make a lasting impression. Whether that impression is good or bad, depends on you. Unfortunately, most of us tend to concentrate on what we want to say rather than on how we sound.

Projecting power doesn't mean preparing a well-thought-through speech, any more than does wearing the right clothes. Executives often affect clipped, staccato-like speech patterns because they feel that suggests the power of their position. They fail to realize that to impart such assurance they need a voice that is resonant, rich, and relaxed. Listen to some of the most successful politicians (whether you agree with their politics or not) and note how convincing a sincere tone can be.

Delivering an address softly can make you sound ineffective and unmotivated. That certainly is not the image you want to project. No matter what the situation, you want to show strength by using a strong voice, speaking in a wide range of tones, and applying some inflection. Your voice discloses a wealth of information about you. A skilled poker face can mask many emotions, but disguising the emotions expressed in your voice is not so simple.

Fear and unhappiness can cause a "lump in the throat" that will interfere with vocal production. And when you feel enthusiastic, you often lose the ability to modulate your voice and you end up pitching it in a higher register. Tension associated with anger or stress will produce harsh, rasping sounds. To ease vocal stress, try yawning before you start speaking. Listen carefully to radio and TV newsreaders and you can easily pick out the strongest, most effective voices. Compare them with the voices of other readers who snuffle words through the nose, speak in a whiney tone, or drone on as though the news is no interest. You can hear the difference in their persuasiveness.

Learn to drop your pitch at the end of a sentence. Ending on an "up" note makes you sound weak and makes the listener feel as though you're seeking agreement. If you get stage fright when speaking to more than a few people, slow your tempo. That will get you breathing on a more regular beat. You'll be more relaxed and you'll be able to communicate more effectively.

If you're not aware of what your voice sounds like to others, check it out with a tape recorder. Read a few paragraphs from a book, then play back the tape. Do you squeak, whine, sound breathy, speak in a monotone? You don't have to live with such drawbacks. You can change your voice or speech patterns with the help of a professional or on your own. And it's not a time-consuming process. You don't have to give up the voice you were born with—just perfect it.

(FK)

STYLES *of* LEARNING

THE FIRE THAT melts the butter hardens the egg. The same thing done by different people is not the same thing. People learn in different ways.

We all know this, in some cranny of our minds, but we have only recently begun to recognize its practical implications. Our schools, our universities, and our corporate training programs too often resemble a bottling plant. Move the empty bottle up, squirt in some math, some poetry, some marketing, some statistics. Cap it, gown it, and send it on its way.

But the world's best learners are pre-schoolers, who charge straight into a project, try, fail, scrape their knees, fall down, cry, and try again. That's how they learn to speak, walk, climb, ride bicycles, negotiate a later bedtime.

For some people hands-on experience is always the easiest route to learning. Others require an analytical, abstract understanding. Some learn best in the morning, others late at night. Some need strong light; some need silence. Teenagers often horrify their parents by working on the floor with the radio or TV blaring. Yet the homework gets done, and new research suggests that some learners need a shell of sound to repel distractions.

The concept of learning styles helps us to understand our own strategies—about which we know more than we realize. Think back to a time when you learned something pleasantly and well. It might be swimming, tying your shoes, skiing, or using a tool. What made that experience special? A lack of pressure, a friendly guide, strong motivation? These may be among your personal requirements for effective learning.

To analyze your learning style more formally, try the model

developed by David Kolb of Case Western Reserve University. (It's published by McBer and Company in Boston.)

Draw a horizontal line. Label the left end "Active Experimentation" and the right end "Reflective Observation." Do you just hop in the new car and drive away? You're an Active Experimenter. If you read the manual first, you're a Reflective Observer.

Now draw a vertical line through the first line. Label the top "Concrete Experience" and the bottom "Abstract Conceptualization." If you start with concrete examples and work your way to general principles, you fit on the upper half of that line. If you need a theoretical overview first, you fall near the bottom. Most people know where they fit along each of these lines. About seven percent of us fall in the upper quadrants, in the "northern" hemisphere. We don't learn easily from readings and lectures; we prefer projects, field trips, and experiments.

But traditional teaching and training are overwhelmingly slanted towards the southern quadrants. What the classroom sells is not what the student wants to buy.

We may someday be able to match each student with a precisely compatible teacher. But we are only beginning to measure and describe learning styles and teaching styles, which also vary tremendously. Nor do we really know whether a "northern" student needs a "northern" teacher at any particular stage or in any specific subject.

Still, the new research shows that any rigid approach will be wrong for many students and that students respond best when we treat them as individuals. As Dr. David Hunt of the Ontario Institute for Studies in Education notes, the theory is really "an attempt to capture what goes on in effective communication."

And communication is the essence of education. Education is something we do with students, not to them. Learning-style research directs our attention to the process, and to the uniqueness of each student. That is no small contribution to the quest for educational excellence.

(SDC)

The JOYS of SOLITUDE

IT'S DIFFICULT TO get away from the daily pressures that surround us. Our privacy suffers from myriad encroachments that impinge on our lives—constant activity, personal relationships, extraneous noise. We are attacked from almost every angle.

We seem to have forgotten how much satisfaction there is in aloneness, how much enjoyment we can find when we escape the constant input. We seem to have overlooked the fact that solitude is an essential ingredient for human growth.

Have you every stopped to think how much we abuse ourselves in the course of our daily lives? There is the dash of deadlines, the millstone of meetings, the requirements of relationships, the tyranny of traffic, the clatter of computers, the turmoil of telephones. Noise surrounds us, swallows us, and smothers us to the point that we have all but forgotten the joys of solitude.

Could it be that the teachings of psychiatry, which posit that a key source of fulfillment is personal relationships, have made us lose sight of our inner selves? Relationships, of course, are vital to human development. But so is solitude.

How do you feel about spending time alone? You realize that being along is different from being lonely. In his book *The Courage to Be*, theologian Paul Tillich wrote, "Our language has wisely sensed the two sides of being alone. It has created the word loneliness to express the pain of being alone. And it has created the word solitude to express the glory of being alone."

There is a virtue in solitude.

Many people have discovered that one of the best ways to come to terms with a traumatic situation is to go off by themselves. The greatest writers, musicians, abstract thinkers, and philosophers have probably led the most solitary lives. There seems to be some connection between the capacity for long periods of concentration on abstract thought and not having the distractions of family or of the business world.

While few of us might choose solitude as a lifelong condition, most of us need at least some time to ourselves. We may differ from our friends, colleagues, and partners in the amount, the frequency, or the urgency of our needs. In fact, we probably differ, too, in the way we spend our time alone. We may have trouble carving out periods of privacy. We may even feel guilty claiming them. But when we're deprived of the pleasures of being alone for too long, we experience distress.

In *Gift From the Sea*, Anne Morrow Lindbergh wrote that "The world today does not understand . . . the need to be alone." She went on to point out that "If one sets aside time for a business appointment, a trip to the hairdresser, a social engagement, that time is accepted as inviolable. But if one says 'I cannot come because that is my hour to be alone,' one is considered rude, egotistical, or strange."

What a sad commentary on our civilization that wanting to be alone is considered suspect; that one has to hide the fact or make excuses as though it were some secret vice.

Take a moment—today—to access your own living patterns. Are you in such a hurry that, as the American author and cleric Peter Marshall once asked, you almost feel as though "you hate to miss one panel of a revolving door?" Slow down and gear back so that there is time for quietness, contemplation, and mediation. Make time for solitude.

(FK)

The TIES THAT BLIND

THAT NECKTIE YOU'RE wearing, gentlemen, what does it disclose about you?

The late American journalist Heywood Broun once wrote that "a necktie ought to have something of rebellion about it." And there are men who reflect that form of self-expression when, each morning, they don one of the ties hanging in their closets. There are plenty of men, on the other hand, who don't particularly want to defy the world. Nonetheless, almost every man does have an opinion—about himself, his job, or his surroundings—that influences the kind of necktie he wears.

Attaching emotional or psychological significance to a necktie—be it sincere, flippant, jolly, gloomy, or whatever—is a notion that has long intrigued social scientists and cultural observers. But saying that the wearer is expressing himself is not the same as saying that anyone who sees a tie can translate its message. The necktie could not have survived this long had it not served some expressive function. After all, its utility is nil! It is uncomfortable in the heat of summer, and a nuisance at any time. Yet many men cling tenaciously to their one remaining pure decoration because it is their only outlet for personal taste and individuality.

Say what you will about a man's suit, his shoes, or the cut of his jib. He will take it calmly. Yet any comment on his tie is likely to be taken as a direct opinion of his personality—and with considerable justification. The tie he wears is there for no reason except that he liked it and chose to wear it . . . for his own reasons. Compliment it, and you make him feel proud of himself in general. Say something disparaging, and you may wound his ego deeply.

That's not to say that ties don't fall prey to fashion. They're wide for a year or two, then fashionably narrow again. They're striped, then patterned, of solid color, then multi-coloured.

Neckties have men by the throat. But suffice it to say that there are no reliable signals about what any particular type of tie means. It was once sneeringly said you should "never trust a man who wears a bow-tie." But no one takes that seriously any more. Winston Churchill wore them, so did Lester Pearson and Harry Truman; the list is endless. Many men still wear them, often to the envy of those who admit they can't tie one.

Some men wear a regular four-in-hand tie, and others prefer them with a heavier Windsor knot. Some sport country-style string ties; others prefer Ivy League plain black knits. No matter how you break down the categories, any attempt to classify a man by his style in neckwear is doomed to confusion and possible disaster.

How do you classify the man who wears his old school tie? Or one with his company logo in an overall design?

Colour may be ambiguous, but the choice between bright and dull is still suggestive. Patterns may be fad-influenced, but however narrow the limits of his choice, a man still has alternatives before him.

A bow-tie is said to have a youthful attitude to it—as much in the way it's tied as in its basic style. Given the other things one can see of a man at first glance—his hair, his suit, the expression on his face—his necktie offers a significant additional clue. If you doubt it, notice your own startled expression the next time you see a tie that looks entirely out of key and don't be surprised when you learn that its wearer got it for Christmas!

(FK)

WHAT TO DO?

FACING DECISIONS IS an everyday occurrence in all of our lives. We usually tackle problems head-on, based either on experience or on what we have known others to do in similar circumstances.

But what do you do when you don't know what to do? How do you cope with a problem that seems unsolvable? What do you do if the dilemma appears utterly impossible, and the more you think about it the more confused you become?

Some people panic. Yet panic is the worst reaction to have. It doesn't allow you to face the predicament with the one important requirement for problem-solving: calm thinking. Panic only creates worry, and that's the surest path to disaster. Worry has never resolved any problems.

Rather than sounding your mental alarm, approach the situation with the knowledge that a solution is not only possible, it is already awaiting you. All problems have solutions—don't forget that. Admitting that you don't know the answer will set you firmly on the road to resolution. Then you can determine what data you need to put you back on the road to making the right decision.

The first thing you might try, especially because it works well for many people, is to sleep on your dilemma. Just before nodding off, think through the various aspects of your predicament step-by-step. You may find upon awakening next morning that the whole mess has become clear in your mind, that the solution is staring you in the face. "Sleeping on it" can also mean putting the problem aside for an hour or two while coping with other business. That can help put your quandary in perspective.

Rather than focusing on the complexity of what is troubling

you, direct your efforts to thinking about the bottom line. This will help you side-step any distracting elements.

Try working backward from the desired result to see how many solutions you can find. Don't be surprised if you end up with more answers than you thought possible. And don't be concerned if some of them seem a little far out. Some of human-kind's greatest ideas have developed out of what were believed to be impracticalities. Solutions that may seem illogical often result in wise decisions.

Nor should you hesitate to seek an outside opinion. Without giving away secrets, you might find that several things happen if you simply verbalize your dilemma to another person. Your confidant may suggest a new perspective. Or you may suddenly see the light when you hear yourself voice your own uncertain-ties. Either way, you're a winner.

Finally, have trust in yourself. Often, when you face what seems insurmountable, you find yourself having an intuitive response. Intuition is really the accumulated experience of years of "doing" rather than sitting on your hands. Some people call it a gut feeling. No matter what you call it, don't dismiss it. You may think you're breaking the rules, but remember that today's problems often cannot be resolved with yesterday's solu-tions. When you hear that little voice telling you to abandon the usual and act on instinct, listen!

As a last resort, if you're still stymied, try to restate your problem in some other way. It could be that the problem isn't what you thought it was. Thinking of it in new words or in other contexts may reflect it in a new light—the true light.

Success depends on mental agility. So when you think you don't know what to do, let yourself become mentally flexible. Listen to what comes to mind first. Laugh if you must . . . and then pause to determine if you haven't just solved your own problem.

(FK)

SO MUCH TO READ

"HOW AM I going to get through all the reading I have to do, and still get around to the books I want to read?"

That's a frequently heard complaint. Despite the fact that we seem to have more leisure than ever before, our time is impinged upon by greater demands of work, study, or "just keeping up."

The major problem seems to be one of impressing on your mind those parts of a book you consider most useful for your own development. You want to have some chance of recalling specific material when you need it. Otherwise, what opportunity do you have of profiting from the valuable things you read?

The purposeful reading of any book requires close attention. The better you concentrate on what you're reading, the more able you are to distinguish between what is important for you to know and what isn't.

The major distraction that seems to bother most readers is daydreaming. William J. Reilly, a noted consultant and researcher, discovered years ago that he could maintain peak attention to any book he was reading for about twenty-five minutes but not much longer.

He experimented by taking a five-minute break when his attention waned. During the break he'd listen to music, or wash his face, or get a drink of water, or just look out of the window and get the daydreaming out of the way. Sometimes he'd walk about the room and whistle. In other words, he took his mind off his book by switching his concentration or just getting to his feet and moving about. After five minutes, he resumed his reading for another twenty-five minutes. His experiment worked.

There are other steps you can take to help you get more out of your books. For example, mark the key passages by underlining them. When you read something that's of particular interest, you are usually confident that you'll "always remember that!" The trouble is, a week later it too often is forgotten. Marking key passages serves two purposes: it underscores in your memory the words you've marked, and it saves precious time later when you review the book.

Some make marginal notes in their books. With pencil in hand, you can record your ideas and comments while they're fresh in your mind. A note made today preserves an observation for future use.

Making a personal index is another habit that will quickly pinpoint material important for your own needs. On the inside back cover of the book, jot down the page numbers you are likely to want to refer to later on. Then you have, at a moment's notice, the best of every book at fingertip command.

Finally, continue to build your own book collection. Make a compilation of books that will be valuable to you. After all, you're entitled to a return on every investment you make. The best way to get tangible returns from the time you invest in books is to build your own tailor-made reference library. And to make sure that these books don't get away from you, place your name and address on the inside front cover of each volume. Then there can be no question about who owns the book, should a well-meaning person borrow it and forget where it came from.

Remember, along with the books you must read, there are many important books you also intend to read—but have never quite found the time for. If you schedule twenty minutes a day at some set hour you'll be amazed how much more good reading you can get done in that short period of concentration.

(FK)

∾

RELAXING YOUR MIND

MARCUS AURELIUS ONCE said that "life is what our thoughts make it." The great Roman emperor and philosopher was warning us that the extent to which we can manage our lives depends on our ability to regulate our thoughts and thus use mental energy efficiently.

Scientists estimate that the brain processes some 50,000 pieces of information a second—that's 180 million items an hour! Your mind is ceaselessly active. In fact, in the few seconds during which you were reading the first paragraph above, many thoughts were probably swirling through your head.

There might have been fleeting anticipation about something you have to do later today. It might surprise you to realize that at the same time as you are worrying about missing a deadline, you may be mulling over ways to improve office efficiency, or ways to redecorate your home, or even agonizing about some remark you regret having made last night.

With all that mental activity going on, how do you eliminate distractions and focus on immediate priorities? The answer lies in a meditative process that some psychologists call "mind quieting." In other words, disregard the distractions of the constantly active thinking process in your head and zero in on your priority target. Mind quieting can help you refocus your energies, whether on some particular task or perhaps on your general health and well-being.

Think of your mind as a radio receiver with thousands of channels, all operating at once. How do you choose a single channel on which to concentrate, while filtering out the "noise" of the other channels?

Proponents of mind quieting suggest taking a little time to close your eyes so that you can vanquish visual distractions, which represent seventy percent of all sensory input. By narrowing sensory input in this way, you can concentrate on sorting through the thousands of thoughts impinging on each other.

Dr. Herbert Benson of the Harvard Medical School suggests that you pick a quiet time, and as quiet a place as you can find. Sit in a straight-backed chair with your eyes shut or only slightly open, he says. Then focus your full attention on the movement of your breath as it enters and leaves your nostrils. Above all, don't try to regulate or control your respiration; just be aware of it. You'll soon find yourself in a quiet, meditative state of awareness.

You may find another method of bringing on this quieted, or centred, state that suits you better. This ability to focus mentally has always been a part of the human capacity, Dr. Benson says, and can be induced both physically and emotionally through such mind-quieting exercises as prayer, yoga, listening to music, or meditation.

The benefits of mind quieting have been scientifically demonstrated in recent years. This form of mental exercise has been used to reduce high blood pressure, to eliminate headaches, to achieve muscular relaxation, even to increase cardiac and respiratory efficiency.

Dr. Benson suggests that you engage in mind quieting at least two or three times a day in periods ranging from five to fifteen minutes—but no longer. Start early in the day, before breakfast, and devote the same amount of time in the late afternoon before dinner. You might also meditate again before bedtime.

Make mind quieting a regular routine for yourself, and you'll quickly perceive positive physical and mental results.

(FK)

SELF-ESTEEM *at* ANY AGE

SELF-ESTEEM MEANS that you feel good about yourself. You feel important in the scheme of things. You know you are an admirable person. It's the only way to go. With a good supply of self-esteem, you can enjoy life; you can conquer the world.

It develops at an early age. A smiling, happy baby, knowing she'll be cared for, reaching out to others, has self-esteem. A child raised on praise, not blame, has it, and feels it grow as he's encouraged to master new skills every day. In youth it's what gets you going; in the middle years it's the nitty-gritty that keeps you going, through triumphs large and small and the odd defeat; in the later years it enables you to relax and enjoy the rest of your life because you know for sure you've earned it.

People of all ages need the esteem of others, too, but if they have a healthy dose of their own, it's more likely they'll receive it.

Unfortunately not everyone possesses this solid feeling of confidence. In some it was never nurtured, or was knocked out of them by others along the way. But there are ways to develop self-esteem, to improve whatever you've got.

First, remember that you are the most important person in the world, at least in your world. This doesn't mean you have to be thoroughly selfish, but without this conviction, you can't even begin to give of yourself to others.

Look as if you are self-confident. It's always worth taking time over your appearance. Attractive clothes, appropriate for the occasion, good grooming of hair and skin, and, for women, becoming makeup, can give you an image of confidence, which is half the battle. Fitness training or the enjoyment of sports can add to your appearance of well-being. Your gestures and posture can project an image of self-confidence, too. Stand tall, not slouched over; lean forward when addressing someone, and speak clearly; smile often, as if looking on the bright side; before long, you will! It's not an affectation; if it's obvious you like yourself, feel you're of some value, others probably will feel the same way about you, too.

Expertise in some line will give you a feeling of confidence, as well as advancing you socially or in a career.

Even if the skill you develop is in another line, perhaps a recreational field, it can pay dividends in your work and social life as well. For instance, an improvement in your tennis game, with the feeling of success it gives you, can be reflected in the determination you show in a work project. Self-confidence is still the name of the game.

Be aware of your own strengths and weaknesses so you can make the most of your good points and cope with your own shortcomings. You'll find that nothing succeeds like success. You do well, receive praise, and are spurred on to do even better. Keep the whole cycle going, starting in a small way and building up to a healthy dose of self-esteem.

By the same token, you can nourish self-esteem in others so they do better work. When people rise to the level of what others expect of them, it's called the Pygmalion effect. When they rise to the level of what they then expect of themselves, they go one better, explains business professor Richard Field of the University of Alberta. They become self-motivated and more demanding of themselves, resulting in higher productivity. It's their self-esteem that does the trick.

(NM)

$\mathcal{O}$

WRITE DOWN THOSE GOALS

DREAMERS FANTASIZE; achievers plan. If you want to achieve anything, plan to achieve it. The very first step is to write down your goal.

Unwritten goals, says time-management consultant Harold Taylor, are not goals at all: they are just "nebulous thoughts. Goals are in writing with completion dates and a plan of action for achieving them." The alternatives to written goals include wishful thinking, memory games, sporadic flurries of activity, guilty resolutions, and similar nervous twitches. The result is not purposive action, but drift.

Genuine goals should be specific, realistic and measurable, and tied to a timetable. By their nature, written goals generate realistic, concrete action plans. Suppose you're a self-employed professional, and your goal is an income of $100,000 a year. Write that down. Does it conflict with other goals? It may: you probably can't take a long vacation in Europe or build your own house while you double your income. Your written goals force you to make realistic choices: which goal has priority; which should be postponed?

Let's say you give priority to your earnings goal. To achieve that, you'll have to earn $8,400 a month, which breaks down to about $2,000 a week or $400 a day. Is that realistic? Can you bill that much every working day without compromising quality? If not, you'll have to make some changes. Perhaps you should improve your time management, raise your rates, or seek a more lucrative niche and a new clientele.

Broken down into its constituent steps, your goal gives you monthly, weekly, and even daily benchmarks. If you billed

$2,500 this week, you can ease off later if need be. In the meantime, enjoy the quiet flush of pride that comes from actually exceeding your interim target. That achievement will bolster your confidence, which is an invaluable asset. With diligence and luck, you can have the pleasure almost every week.

Write down personal and family goals in the same way. Don't be cowed by your present circumstances: write down your deepest desires. If you aren't going to satisfy them in this lifetime, when are you going to do it? Never mind how unlikely it sounds. If you really want to be a beachcomber, a banker, or a bishop, write that down.

Once again, the written goal generates a plan. Research the steps you'll have to take to achieve that goal. Decide which steps come first, and which are the most important ones. Set a timetable, with the high-priority items first. Maybe you'll have to go back to university. Very well: estimate the cost and start looking for bursaries and loans. Write down every step you can think of and set a deadline for each one. Cross it off the list when you've completed it.

Most goals are more modest. Perhaps you want to play the piano, build model airplanes with your children, become a municipal councillor. Now write it down with a measurable definition of success: Toronto Conservatory grade two in a year's time, one model airplane a month. How many hours, all told, will it take to achieve that? Which hours will you set aside for that activity? Block off those hours on your planning calendar, starting this week. If you don't schedule those hours, you'll never find them.

Writing out your goals helps you to see that large goals are achieved in stages. You write a book one page at a time, build a fence one board at a time. In 1921, at fifty-six, Harry Pidgeon and his home-built yawl *Islander* completed a four-year single-handed circumnavigation of the world. He was the second man in history to do so. When an admirer marvelled at the feat,

Pidgeon shrugged. "You know how to sail one day by yourself, don't you?" Pidgeon asked. "Well, that's all it is—just one day after another."

(SDC)

The USES *of* PROPHECY

ONE DAY IN the 1870s, a Polish girl named Marya was running down the road with her friends. An old gypsy woman stopped her and demanded to see her hand. The other girls tried to persuade Marya to leave, but the old gypsy held fast to her hand, excitedly describing the remarkable lines on her palm and predicting she would become famous. She was right: Marya moved to France, became a scientist, and is known to history as Madame Marie Curie.

Did the gypsy really know the future? Our sceptical age finds it easier to believe that she shaped it by implanting that dramatic image of the future into a little girl's mind. But that process is almost as awesome—and it can make a potent tool for parents and managers. The eminent psychiatrist R.D. Laing calls the process "attribution," and considers it a supremely powerful technique for influencing people. The best way to get someone to be what one wants him to be, says Laing, is "not to tell him what to be, but to tell him what he is. Such attributions, in context, are many times more powerful than orders."

These "attributions" are actually prophecies: statements designed to foretell, and thus to mould the future. Shape a person's expectations, and you shape that person's actions. And no wonder. All of our achievements—and many of our mistakes—exist first as ideas, and only later as objects or actions.

So expectations that are treated as fact very often become fact. Indeed, our expectations can determine whether we live or die. People who have not prepared for a rewarding retirement often die within months of their golden handshake, while others who

123

take retirement as a creative opportunity often seem as robust in their eighties as they did in their sixties.

We have all experienced the power of attribution and prophecy. Parents often use it: "You're a good girl," we say, and eventually the little stinker actually does behave decently. When General MacArthur stood at Bataan and declared, "I shall return," he took the first long step towards doing so. All sales reps know the importance of an unshakeable conviction that a product is good and that they can sell it. Good salespeople often use attribution when closing a sale, too. "Shall I have it delivered or will you take it with you?" they ask, thus attributing a purchase decision to the customer.

But we often do these things by instinct and imitation, without a clear grasp of the principles. People who use prophecy consciously and effectively, however, become powerful teachers, supervisors, and mentors.

Such people don't harangue their subordinates, their students, or their children. Instead, they wait until they catch other people doing things right, and then applaud the performance. By the same token, they respond to errors not with annoyance or resignation, but with surprise. "That's not like you at all," they say. "A person as capable as you wouldn't normally make such a mistake."

The technique is equally effective when we apply it to ourselves. Great achievers in every field are marked by a conviction of their own destiny, whether or not anyone shares it. They develop that belief by focusing intently on their goals, by imagining the experience of success, and by telling themselves over and over, day after day, that they can and will reach those goals. The world may see an obscure Toronto reporter or a struggling salesman, but within the reporter lurks a great novelist, within the salesman is a future tycoon. Both stories are true: the reporter was Ernest Hemingway, and the salesman was Roy Thomson.

Their counterparts exist today, utterly sure of the greatness within them. Those people are the household names of tomorrow.

(SDC)

The MYSTERY *of* CONFIDENCE

CONFIDENCE IS A crucial factor in professional success—more important, often, than skill, charm, or even intelligence. Without confidence, we cannot manage, sell, negotiate, hire, or fire. In private life we need confidence to marry, buy a house, have a child.

Yet confidence remains the most mysterious of indispensable qualities. It sometimes arrives as an unexpected blessing, as startling and welcome as a sunbeam piercing a canopy of clouds. It can vanish just as quickly, a wraith of smoke dissipated on an almost imperceptible breeze. Fortified by confidence, we can do astonishing things. Sabotaged by its absence, we are almost incapable of action.

What can we do to bolster our self-confidence?

If we have lost it, can we regain it?

Yes, absolutely. Employ these proven techniques:

• Value your own achievements. You've passed innumerable tests already, from riding a bike to passing university exams. Don't discount those achievements: they're all challenges you've met and passed, and they're the best possible evidence that you'll succeed again in the future. Try writing a private résumé of your successes from childhood on. Include the moments when you felt proud, happy, fulfilled. Does the résumé portray a person you'd want for a friend? Good: you should be your own friend.

• Listen to those who love you. Your children admire you, your spouse is happy to be married to you, your friends enjoy your company. They aren't fools, are they? You'd accept their opinions on other subjects: shouldn't you accept their good opinion of you?

• Count your successes, not your failures. If only five percent of prospects actually buy the product you're selling, you'll be rejected nineteen times out of twenty. If you dwell on those rejections, you'll tumble into depression. But hey, you sold two of those things last week and that's terrific!

• Manage your challenges. Pick challenges you can meet, and give yourself the experience of success, but make each challenge a little tougher than the last one. The Greek hero Milo lifted the same calf off the ground every day. At the end of a year, he was lifting a bull.

• Prepare carefully. Before the big meeting, do extra research. Nothing gives more confidence than the knowledge that the facts really are on your side. Dress appropriately: the good impression you create will be reflected back to you. Rehearse your presentation: if you know it cold, you can concentrate on making a brilliant delivery.

• Nourish your sense of humour. The sense of humour is really a sense of proportion. Was your gaffe that important? Did his insult really matter? If you make a fool of yourself and laugh about it, you draw the sting from your failure and endear yourself to others.

• Set your own terms. Don't dwell on the past: it's gone and can't be changed. But what are your goals for the future? Social service? Wealth? A happy family? Define success in your own terms, and don't worry about "failures" in areas that aren't among your priorities. The best goals are processes: developing a skill, building a happy marriage, mastering a field of knowledge. Such goals lead a person to concentrate not on a distant result, but on an immediate daily experience of growth and competence.

• Take action. Above all, don't mope or dither: act. Slice the problem into manageable pieces, and attack the first piece now. You'll make mistakes, but mistakes are the stepping-stones of learning. The worst mistake of all is to sit there paralysed by your own insecurity.

(SDC)

IV

FAMILY

TIES

❦

SUPERB TEACHERS

"THE SUCCESSFUL TEACHER today is really a coach," confides Winnipeg teacher Norman Lee. "The good teacher is the guide on the side, not the sage on the stage."

Norman Lee is one of twelve Canadian teachers (one from each province and territory) who received Marshall McLuhan Distinguished Teacher Awards last spring. Conferred by the Marshall McLuhan Centre for Global Communications and supported by such substantial corporate sponsors as Telecom Canada, Dofasco, Molson, Volkswagen, and Xerox, the McLuhan Awards are an overdue recognition of Canada's finest teachers.

The winners are beacons of hope—leaders in a profound transformation of our schools.

Today's outstanding educators teach concepts more than content, process more than product. "The relationship between student and teacher has changed more dramatically than anything else in my time as a teacher," notes John McCarthy of Newcastle, New Brunswick.

In Laval, Quebec, students working with Claude Dignard have created an aerospace complex, including a working space-shuttle simulator. In Yarmouth, Nova Scotia, Kenneth Langille's students simulate courtroom trials using a computer database called MacLAW, created right in the school. In Iqaluit, Northwest Territories, John Jamieson's students are doing original research on the parasites that infest the community's dogs. In Radville, Saskatchewan, Thérése Durston publishes *Kid Proof*, a nationally circulated magazine written by and for children between the ages of six and thirteen.

Almost all of these top teachers make powerful and imaginative use of the new technology. In Graeme Wilson's technology education program in Rosedale, British Columbia, students do creative work with laser optics and holography. Joyce Sward's mass-media course in Whitehorse integrates desktop publishing with practice in video, photo-journalism, advertising, and reporting.

Students in Russell Bragg's classroom in Roberts Arm, Newfoundland, create computer-generated animation on videotape, while every grade three in Gloria Cathcart's Edmonton classroom has an Apple computer, linked to seventy schools around the world through the Apple Global Education Network.

Electronic mail gives them an immediate, worldwide audience. "Children around the world have so much in common," Cathcart remarks. "We put the first lines of some couplets out on the system, and asked other schools to complete them. We got responses from Norway, Spain, New Mexico, Baffin Island, and Massachusetts—and their second lines were very much like what my students had written in the first place."

But the innovative classroom can be demanding. Richard Ford, an art and music teacher in Willowdale, Ontario, insists that student projects "must involve something new, must involve a risk, and must end with a written self-evaluation. What problems did you confront? How were they solved? What mark would you give yourself?" Ford doesn't necessarily accept the evaluations: some kids, he says, mark themselves far too hard.

Charlottetown's Len Sirois points out that his best students have devoted, disciplined parents. "Kids need their parents to help them set goals," Sirois explains. "You need your parents to tell you what's really important, to remind you that education is what you carry with you all your life."

Superb teachers can help children blossom, but parents are the earth in which they are rooted. The finest blossoms, it seems, still grow from the most solidly rooted plants.

(SDC)

ce

TIME *at* HOME

MORE AND MORE Canadians are finding themselves working longer hours. The generally accepted thirty-five- or forty-hour week is too often a stranger in the executive suite and to middle managers. As good as dedication to job and future may be for a career, it's bound to play havoc with home life.

Worse, not getting home until seven or eight p.m. most week-days is a sure formula to damage relationships with spouse and offspring; it's a sure way to destroy a family. With the business world now more fast-paced than ever, it is vital to separate one's professional from one's private life.

There are undoubtedly a lot of things you would like to do in your leisure time, but you probably never get around to them. The solution is to plan. And the key to planning your time at home is to effect a balance of timing: not so much planning that you feel you're on the job, and not so little that you fail to accomplish what is important to you.

In achieving this balance, make a conscious effort to change your mind-set when you're not at work. If you make a firm agenda of what to do before going out to spend a Saturday afternoon with your children, it's a sure sign that your head is still at the office. To break such rigidity of thinking, establish some physical clues that will help you separate office time.

For example, try not to wear a watch on weekends. If you feel time pressures even when you're at home, don't use digital clocks in your home or in your car; they pace off the seconds and minutes far too relentlessly for the work-driven person. Change your clothes the minute you get home from the office. If there's office work that must be done in the evening, make a place for it physically—the lone spot in the house in which work will be appropriate. Don't spread papers out on the couch or dining room table. Don't take business reading to bed with you.

Relax before plunging into housework or domestic activities. If you have to make dinner when you get home from the office, take a ten-minute break after you get in the door. It can make all the difference as to whether you'll experience the rest of the evening as a pleasure or as a pressure.

Above all, resist the tendency to abuse the whole winding-down process by indulging in activities that create problems of their own: compulsive sex, addictive exercise, overindulgence in food and/or drink, or the use of recreational drugs.

Use the transitional time between office and home as a period of discovery: drive or walk home along a different route; pick up something new at the newsstand instead of the usual evening newspaper.

The quality of the time you spend with your mate is just as important as the quality in everything else. Don't limit conversation to terse exchanges of information. Speak in a way that conveys interest, involvement, a sense of love. Learn to appreciate a little physical contact—a pat, a hug—especially during stressful times.

If you can learn to leave the office behind—not necessarily every day, but most days—then you will have achieved the same balance that you have at work, where you have busy seasons and slack seasons. You might find that a little ritual at the end of the business day will help you switch from work mode to home mode. For example, before leaving the office, try making a list of things that need to be done the next day. Or do something as simple as turning over the page on your daily calendar.

Remember that no one ever said on his or her deathbed, "I wish I had spent more time at the office."

(FK)

YOU & YOUR PARENTS

YOUR RELATIONSHIP WITH your children is just one face of the coin. The other side? The relationship you have as an adult "child" with your elderly parents. As the human life cycle continues to lengthen, parent-child relationships grow longer and often more troublesome.

For one thing, there is the adult child's guilt when parents disapprove of what they do. Then there is the frustration when parents don't understand the problems of the younger generations. And, finally, adult children often resent letting their parents have their own way, even though they sense that this attitude is wrong.

Just as living with adult children can be stressful for parents, having parents living with them can be stressful for the adult children. Yet, odd though it may seem, the greatest problems exist when the children and parents don't share the same living quarters. In those circumstances, the adult children become reluctant to visit the elderly parents, particularly when the family relationship has been ridden with conflict.

As they age, problem parents become more of a problem. The parent who has always managed to provoke guilt in an offspring by being excessively demanding, or by continually playing the martyr's role, will prove to be even more demanding and guilt-provoking in old age.

The threat to their own mortality becomes apparent to the offspring as they themselves get older and have a front-row view of their parents becoming aged and infirm. There is also the fact that the parent-child role gets reversed as the parents age. The dependency and frailty of older parents—whether physical or psychological—makes many of them assume childlike roles. The adult children, in turn, experience a sharp loss because they recognize that they can no longer turn to their parents.

Psychologist Dr. Howard Halpern says that however enraged or frustrated you are by a parent's behaviour, you must learn to accept the role reversal that has taken place. Your parents are now actually dependent and helpless in some ways; they are not the same antagonists you remember from early-childhood conflicts.

You should try to make regular visits to your parents so that they can look forward to your arrival and plan for it. If you are planning an extended trip, it's a good idea to inform your parents of your return date, tell them when they can expect to hear from you, and even how they can make contact with you should that become necessary.

It's important that you not visit your parents at the expense of your own adult priorities. Excessive guilt often pushes children into running themselves ragged visiting parents too often. And be sensitive to the fact that some parents lead busy, extremely independent lives and may not want too many visits from adult children.

Be aware that too much indulgence of parental wishes, or treating parents like infants, can impair the parents' will to continue assuming responsibility for their own lives. Avoid placating behaviour; this is a hangover from the childhood relationship. A realistic and caring attitude is better.

During your visits listen to your parents' problems, but also try sharing concerns of your own—if they are not overwhelming. You should give your parents the respect they deserve by offering them the opportunity to give advice and exercise authority.

(FK)

❦

YOUR UNDERACHIEVING CHILD

WHEN YOU AND your spouse walk in the door at six o'clock, your daughter is talking on the phone while she watches television, her schoolbag lying unopened on the floor. She hasn't done a tap of homework. She's bright, but she just scrapes by. She even says she'd just as soon fail. Your daughter is an "underachiever"—a student whose academic performance does not reflect her abilities. What can be done to help such kids, especially by parents who themselves are overworked and short of time?

Kids become underachievers for a variety of reasons, says York University's Dr. Harvey Mandel, author of *The Psychology of Underachievement*. Underachievement often starts with "an event, or a constellation of events—immigration, a death in the family, divorce, a sudden change in the family's financial circumstances, that sort of thing." The crisis makes school unimportant, and that perception lingers even after the crisis has passed.

Bright children may find school genuinely boring, and simply tune out. Other students are desperately afraid of classroom competition, unable to use their small failures as the launching pad for new successes. Still others may have been terrorized by scornful or sarcastic teachers, or been labelled as "emotionally disturbed" or "learning disabled."

Such problems are not deep-seated. "With more stubborn problems," says Dr. Esther Cole, senior psychologist at the Toronto Board of Education, "you really need to look at family dynamics." Families with long-term, deeply rooted conflicts, for instance, offer children plenty of room to manoeuvre and manipulate. Single parents, by contrast, find it easy to overindulge and overprotect, allowing the child's wishes to dominate family life.

Either way, the child becomes addicted to attention, and expects the rest of the world—including the school—to continue providing personal service, untrammelled freedom, and unearned applause. The school system, alas, reserves its applause for disciplined effort and concrete results—and the child withdraws.

What can parents do to break the cycle of underachievement? Dr. Cole stresses the importance of strong ties between school and home. Parents and teachers need to share a consistent strategy, and communicate steadily.

Parents should also try to find out what's really going on in the child's life at school, with peers, in after-school activities. It takes time to build up trust, but the time is well spent. If need be, call in a professional mediator—a psychologist, teacher, or social worker—to kick-start the communication.

Dr. Cole also suggests that teachers and parents concentrate on helping students with study skills and work habits. The crucial objective is to develop good academic strategies, to help the child learn how to learn.

In *The Underachievement Syndrome*, Dr. Sylvia Rimm recommends a point system for homework, which can be put in the form of a contract. Award one point for each page read, three points for each page written, five points for a page of math homework properly completed, and so on. Working steadily, a student can earn twenty to twenty-five points per hour and use them for a skateboard, a computer game, or a weekend trip. The point system gives immediate benefits to the student.

Parents are vitally important as models of good work habits, too. If you love your work and do it wholeheartedly, you're showing the intrinsic rewards of effort. But your child has to know about your work, and your joy in it. So talk about it, or let your child see you do it.

Above all, keep your sense of humour and proportion. You're doing this because you love your child. The problem and your responses shouldn't mask the love: they should enhance it.

(SDC)

SAFETY *in* THE HOME

ALMOST FIFTEEN PERCENT of accidents in this country occur within the safe confines of the home. That disclosure, recently made public by Statistics Canada, has brought to light the fact that danger lurks almost everywhere in your own house. Fire can burn and kill. Electricity can shock. Hot water can scald. A slippery surface can cause a fall. Knives can cut. The list is endless.

Unfortunately, most accidents are caused by ignorance, carelessness, selfishness, or impatience. And most, if not all, accidents can be prevented. Obviously, there is no immunity from danger. In his recently published book, *The M&S Home Emergency Handbook & First-Aid Guide*, Fred Kerner points out that while your home is the single most dangerous place in which you find yourself daily, most people take the view that "Inasmuch as my home is my castle, it must offer the ultimate in safety." The truth is, the author states, that your home is a dangerous domain. And, sadly, too few people are willing to think of, let alone prepare for, the day when an emergency might strike.

Studies made by the Canada Safety Council indicate that seventy-five percent of all domestic accidents are preventable. So the responsibility for developing a safety plan for your home falls directly on the shoulders of the adults living there. It's up to them to remove all possible hazards, and also to make sure that every member of the family understands how to participate in preventive action should an emergency occur.

The first fundamental in safeguarding your home is good housekeeping: cleanliness and orderliness. Loose objects should not be left on stairs, floors, or landings; floors should not be allowed to remain wet or greasy after a spill has occurred; sharp utensils or tools should not be left lying around when they are not in use lest they be inadvertently handled or even touched, especially by tiny, curious hands.

Interestingly, most home fatalities are the result of accidents in bedrooms and bathrooms. Smoking in bed, careless handling of electric plugs, loose rugs, and clothing left where it can be tripped over are among the leading trouble-makers in the bedroom. In the bathroom, the tub is too often a deceptively slippery place. And the medicine cabinet not only contains such sharp objects as razor blades, but also—temptation to curious youngsters—pills and other medicines that can be ingested easily and with disastrous results.

Stairwells, the kitchen, and even the garden are also culprits and claim their share of the accidents and fatalities. Yet it requires only a little time to survey your home. Just as factories have safety committees, why not your home? Bring the family together and brainstorm the problem: how can you avoid accidents? Review your findings every six months or so.

When people have escaped injury in an accident, they should take the time to analyze what happened. That's the best way to avoid the same danger in the future. The first question to ask yourself after you become involved in an accident is: "How did it happen?" It doesn't matter whether the accident is a little one, like a cut finger, or a big one, like a broken bone; find the answer to "how," and you are forearmed against a repetition.

It does no good to preach safety in a broad, grave, general way. You have to pin-point household safety as a personal obligation. In the midst of household appliances, poisons, fires, and other hazards, your well-being can be at risk every hour of the day. It is only good sense, in this environment, to become not only accident fearing but also safety conscious.

Remember, your own safety is up to you.

(FK)

The STATE *of* YOUR UNION

MARRIED COUPLES TEND to spend so much time apart these days that the little time they do have together tends to lose the richness it once had for them. Young couples, particularly, forced into a two-income situation, forget that the quality of time they spend together is as important as quality in everything else.

A key ingredient to a happy marriage is good communication. Instead of speaking to each other in a way that conveys interest and involvement—a sense of love—you may find that your conversation has become a terse exchange of information. To weather the usual stresses of any close, long-lived relationship, experts recommend a four-point approach to overcoming poor interchanges of ideas.

First, always be specific whether praising or criticizing the actions of your spouse. Vague complaints are bound to trigger arguments.

Second, during an argument with your spouse, don't revive grudges of long ago, or recall examples of past misbehaviour.

Third, learn to identify statements or actions that you are consciously aware have very often led to escalating hostility between you. The moment you catch yourself in such a scene, stop everything and cool down. Remember that once these processes build up momentum, they're almost always impossible to stop.

And last, though far from least, edit statements that needlessly hurt your spouse even if they are true.

It's important that you never hesitate to show affection for one another—and that doesn't mean only during sexual interludes. Discover the joys of a little physical contact, especially during very hectic or stressful periods of your life. Don't be hesitant to touch each other, whether it's while you're shopping together or just working around the house. It's important to let each other know that you like one another.

Plan and share activities from which you both can benefit. Perhaps you can redecorate a room, or take tennis or golf lessons. Cook a meal together once in a while, or work in the garden. Don't find yourself considering that non-work is a void that has to be filled with more work.

Verbalize those aspects of your personality that aren't apparent in your daily life. Don't be afraid to talk about your deepest desires and feelings. For instance, why not share sexual fantasies?

Ask yourselves some introspective questions and compare notes on your answers. For example:
• Do you listen to each other?
• Do you have differences over the control, spending, saving, or making of money?
• Do you share friends, or do you each have your own?
• Do you have friends of the opposite sex and, if so, does this cause problems?

Sharing answers to questions such as these provides an enlightened way of learning to communicate better with each other. And should a fight develop—as well it may from time to time—remember to always fight fair. Develop your own rules of combat. Never attack your spouse's one weakness—that's usually a defenseless spot. And stick to the subject; don't confuse the matter with anger that results from some other problem between you.

Above all, keep your fights strictly verbal. A fight that turns physical will inevitably intimidate rather than resolve. And, should you become tempted, remember that the law is finally taking a jaundiced look at spouse beating.

(FK)

∞

FULL-TIME PARENTS
at HOME

THESE DAYS WHEN it's the norm for both parents to be working, mothers who stay home to care for their kids may feel that their kind is becoming an endangered species. For their part, fathers at home, whose numbers are even fewer, may still feel that they're blazing a trail.

According to Statistics Canada, 65.9 percent of women whose youngest child is under thirteen are in the labour force. Of mothers whose youngest children are under three, 58.3 percent are working. With children aged three to five, 65.1 percent work, and by the time their youngest children are between six and twelve, 72.6 percent are gainfully employed.

Although a career for a woman is considered important, it isn't always by choice that mothers return to work. More often it's because two incomes are needed to raise a family. There are also some mothers, used to a stimulating work environment, who'd feel stifled if they were at home with young children all day. Still others, mostly professionals who have invested years of training in their careers, can't let the crucial years slip by without sacrificing advancement in their field.

Mothers at home have weighed the pros and cons, including the cost of going to work in terms of daycare, transportation, clothing, lunches, and many extras, and have opted for home-making. Some have the best of both worlds, either part-time work or work done at home, and as more of such work becomes available, their numbers will grow. Many mothers at home, particularly during their children's early childhood, take courses, get involved in the community, or pursue some hobby that

141

exercises their talents and gives them the adult stimulation they need.

Some fathers stay at home by choice, thanks to paternity leave, or because it's their wives who most need or want to work. There are still others on shift work who have free time to care for the children during the day, giving them a chance to share in their children's nurturing.

Most parents-at-home are grateful that they are able to be there, thankful that they can watch their babies and children grow, be there for the first smile, the first words, the first step. Later, as their children get older, they're glad to be on hand when the kids come home from school, waving their art work, talking about the adventures of the day, and glad they can cope when something goes wrong.

Stay-at-home mothers often find they are picking up the slack for working mothers. They take their children in carpools to outside activities, look after them on teachers' professional development days, and sometimes are called to the school in a crisis when the children's parents can't be reached. They do have some sympathy for the working mothers. "I bet a lot of them would give anything to be able to stay at home with their children," said one. "I'm just lucky I can."

In the meantime, at-home parents sometimes feel like non-persons. "What do you do?" is a frequent question at gatherings, since people define themselves largely by their work. "Well, I'm a homemaker," or "I'm at home with my kids," they reply. Frequently their questioner continues probing with "Well, what did you do *before*?" leaving them with the impression that their present career is of no interest.

But most full-time mothers feel they have an important job at home. They look with interest at successful women in their forties and fifties who are enjoying a second career, and are enriched by the time they spent with their children.

(NM)

∽

SUMMER CAMPS

IN ARICHAT, NOVA Scotia, young Edgar Samson of Premium Sea-foods proudly shows off his company's new high-tech freezer. Samson is happy: the freezer makes his company competitive.

Canada is the world's largest exporter of fish, but we import processing equipment from tiny Denmark. We export logs and import chain saws. Our coal-miners use German machinery.

What can we do about Canada's vanishing industrial base? Science, technology, innovation, and knowledge are the driving forces of today's industrial economy, but Canada's research and development spending is less than half that of our key competi-tors. We have ninety scientists and researchers per 100,000 peo-ple; Japan has 240, and the United States has 280. We face a shortage of 30,000 engineers within a decade, but university enrolments in science and technology are dropping.

Some organizations are bravely bucking the trend. High-tech companies like IBM, Digital, Unisys, and Xerox spend tens of millions of dollars on education, both in the educational system and in-house. The federally funded Canada Scholarships Pro-gram now offers $2,000 a year to 2,500 undergraduates in sci-ence and engineering. And some private foundations are carrying the issues directly to Canadian teenagers.

Among the most effective are two unique summer camps. They are Shad Valley Summer Program and Monkey Business, run by the Waterloo-based Canadian Centre for Creative Tech-nology and designed to attract young people to careers in sci-ence, technology, and business.

In 1990, 400 grade eleven and twelve students took part in the Shad Valley Summer Program, a month-long residential camp held at eight universities from British Columbia to Nova Scotia. The students were chosen on the basis of academic achievement, creativity, initiative, and interpersonal skills.

Shad Valley's daily schedule typically includes lectures on math, computer science, engineering, and entrepreneurship, mixed with projects and seminars on robotics, computer-aided design and manufacturing, bioengineering, solar energy, and similar topics. The program is augmented by speakers from industry, government, and the academic world.

Each group is guided by four university professors and six graduate students who live in residence with the students during the program. Shad Valley is stimulating and intense, but it also includes barbecues, trips to businesses, camping and rafting expeditions, dances, and other recreational activities.

Most Shad Valley participants have corporate sponsors and, over the years, more than twenty companies have participated, including AirCreebec, BCTel, Dofasco, Falconbridge, Canfor, and Federal Industries. Sponsors pay about $3,500, and many sponsored students spend part of the summer in paid employment with their sponsoring companies. Sponsored students also pay a fee of $500, which allows CCCT to accept unsponsored students at a fee of $1,750.

Monkey Business is a one-week mini-Shad directed at students in grades seven and eight, instituted for the first time in 1990 at the University of Calgary and the University College of Cape Breton. It aims to show young people "the excitement inherent in business, science, and technology . . . in an environment where fun, friendship, and recreation are also highly valued." Its $500 cost is normally borne by parents, though some bursaries are available.

Parents and sponsors are delighted—and so are the students. Shad Valley, says one, "is absolutely and without question the best thing I have ever done in my whole entire life." Our children need tools, opportunities, and inspiration. For a lucky few, at least, these programs provide them.

(SDC)

The SANDWICH GENERATION

A WAY OF LIFE that all but vanished a generation or two ago is slowly reappearing. At the same time as our lifespan is lengthening, a generational lifestyle is being revived. Many families today consist of adults in mid-life, the central players in our drama, being depended upon by aging, emotionally reliant, financially needy parents as well as by adult offspring who are often also in less-than-healthy financial straits.

The lead players in this tragicomedy, the one-time baby boomers, are now the Sandwich Generation. Having reached the fortysomething stage, they find themselves caught up in a life pattern that society has almost completely forgotten how to cope with. And the situation is destined to spread. Statistics Canada estimates that thirteen percent of the citizenry will be older than sixty-five within the next ten years. And by the year 2020, a little more than a generation away, the proportion will have risen to about eighteen percent.

What the Sandwich Generation faces is, for them, an uncharted way, a lifestyle their forebearers experienced as normal. It revolves around offspring still living at home—or having had to move back in due to recessionary times—and parents no longer able to cope for themselves in their own homes.

The two-generational nuclear family of the twentieth century is being supplanted by the re-emerging three-generational family of the nineteenth. The two younger generations now have to learn afresh the ways of living within the larger family unit. In the past, when families were not of the sociologically planned one- and two-offspring type that developed after World War II, an extra pair of adults in the home (the grandparents) was not an added burden. They often proved a boon: built-in babysitters or, in a way, second sets of parents. But the Sandwich Generation generally didn't grow up within such families. They haven't experienced the ways of coping with this phenomenon. Nor have their children, especially those who are themselves adults. The result is that the two nuclear generations that originally shared living space now have to learn to adjust to a new way of life, as does the older generation.

The Sandwich Generation is quickly discovering that people grow older in the same way. Not having grown up in a home with grandparents, they've found that some "elders" live healthy, active, and productive lives on their own. They are not a burden. Others require a small amount of assistance in their daily activities though still living at home. And a third group requires constant care in an institution, but that's a potential problem of another stripe.

Caring for the elderly can have many rewards. It can also bring just as many frustrations, especially if you are ill-prepared to run interference for the two age-disparate segments of your family.

It's important to remember that you have to balance the relationships in parallel terms. You, getting along with a younger generation, are still considered the "younger generation" by your parents. All three generations have to cope, but the Sandwich Generation, caught in the middle, has to lead the way. Having two generations living in the same home can be stressful. With three, the stress can be exponential.

You and your offspring must recognize that your elders have come through traumatic changes in their lifetimes. They have much to offer; they merit our care, admiration, and love. If you play your cards the right way, the experience can be rewarding for all of you.

(FK)

The INESTIMABLE VALUE *of* PETS

MAYBE WE SHOULDN'T have been surprised when it was discovered.

Back in the late 1970s, archaeologists working in the Middle East came across a human skeleton, more than 10,000 years old, with its hand lying over the bones of a puppy.

Herbert Spencer, the nineteenth-century English philosopher, possibly put it best: "The behaviour of men to the lower animals, and their behaviour to each other bear a constant relationship." But we don't really need archaeological digs or brilliant essayists to tell us what most of us have known since our childhood. Pets have been an important part of human existence since long before the Sumerian and Babylonian peoples kept leopards, monkeys, and yes, even cats and dogs, as beloved pets.

What is far newer is the growing amount of scientific data that consistently proves the profound importance of pets in the very notional and physical survival of we humans.

Guide dogs for the blind have long been part of our societies; even the ancient Romans used them. Far more recent, however, are such wonders as the furry graduates of Hearing Ear Dogs of Brantford, Ontario, used by the hearing-impaired for everything from alerting them to a ringing phone, a smoke alarm blast, or a simple knock at the door.

But you need not have a disability in order to desire a pet, as the North American owners of some 270 million fish, 60 million cats, 55 million dogs, 50 million birds, and more than 130 million gerbils, turtles, snakes, frogs, and other animals would readily agree. Indeed, research suggests that the real disabilities belong to those who choose not to have a pet.

As early as 1979, a University of Manitoba survey of ninety-eight Canadian child-care residential facilities showed that sixty-five percent of them were using, or planning to use, animals as part of their programs. And how could they not? Study after study across North America has shown that teaching children to care for an animal enhances their social skills. "It made the children more cooperative and sharing," said one psychologist.

So much for kids; how about we adults? You won't be shocked to discover that blood pressure almost always rises when two people talk to one another. "In contrast," explained psychiatrist Aaron Katcher at a Pets in Society symposium held in Toronto several years ago, "when people speak to their pets, their blood pressure remains the same or even drops." The reason is obvious, and was given by author George Eliot more than a century ago: "Animals are such agreeable friends. They ask no questions, pass no criticism."

And as for the sick and elderly, the evidence is irrefutable: pets keep us going. One of the most famous studies was made by the above Dr. Katcher and others, in 1977, of ninety-two heart patients who had been discharged from hospital a year earlier: the mortality rate among the ex-patients who lived with pets was only one-third as great as those without a dog or cat. With the evidence so black and white, it's no wonder that the Winnipeg Humane Society, for the past ten years, has assisted more than 100 volunteers in taking some 200 puppies and kittens every week to spend an hour with people living in seniors' residences or personal-care homes. Such visits to shut-ins "have proven invaluable" to the health and happiness of the recipients, said Deborah McTaggart-Baird, the Society's volunteer coordinator, this past spring.

The value of pets is so clear, in fact, that the reticence of some to their therapeutic use enrages some experts. University of Toronto psychology professor Dr. Barney Gilmore once lashed out, "A city that will not allow its elderly to have pets is killing old people."

(AG)

V

READING

LIST

❧

WORKADAY WISDOMS

Counteracting Jet Lag

Kowet, Don. *The Jet Lag Book: How to reset your mind and body and beat the fatigue of jet lag*. Crown, 1983.

Stewart, Gordon W. *Things Your Travel Agent Never Told You: A traveler's survival guide to health, fitness and worry-free travel*. Grosvenor House, 1983.

"Circadian Rhythms—or We've All Got Rhythm," *Health News*, University of Toronto Faculty of Medicine, 5:4.

The Manners of Mobility

Martin, Judith. *Miss Manners' Guide to Excruciatingly Correct Behavior*. Warner Books, 1983.

"Cellular Phones Gain Support as Technology Takes Hold," *Mobile Electronics*, September 1989.

"Talk to Me, Baby," *Rolling Stone*, May 18, 1989.

"Phones to Go," *Toronto Star*, Saturday, November 19, 1988.

Good Health at Work

Ainsworth, Thomas H. and Michael P. O'Donnell, Eds. *Health Promotion in the Workplace*. John Wiley & Sons, 1984.

Boutilier, Marie, Martin Shain, Helen Suurvali, Eds. *Healthier Workers: Health promotion and employee assistance programs*. Lexington Books, 1986.

Carver, Virginia and Charles Ponee, Eds. *Women, Work and Wellness*. The Addiction Research Foundation of Ontario, 1989.

Fitness and Lifestyle at the Workplace. Fitness and Amateur Sport. Government of Canada, 1988.

Going It Alone

Adler, William. *Chance of a Lifetime*. Warner Books, 1985.

Davidson, Jeffrey P. *Avoiding the Pitfalls of Starting Your Own Business*. Walker & Company, 1988.

Maul, Lyle and Dianne Mayfield. *The Entrepreneur's Road Map*. Saxtons River Publications, 1990.

Mirabella, Marima. *Changing the Rules*. Stoddard, 1988.

Art in the Office

Arts Atlantic magazine

C Magazine

Canadian Art magazine

Parachute magazine

Ethics of Conservation

Agenda For Action:—A report on business and the environment: an ethical solution. Canadian Centre for Ethics and Corporate Policy, Toronto.

Evernden, Neil. *The Natural Alien: Environmentalism and World View.* University of Toronto Press, 1985.

Management Ethics, the newsletter of the Canadian Centre for Ethics and Corporate Policy, Toronto.

WARMER (World Action for Recycling Materials & Energy from Rubbish) International Bulletin, United Kingdom.

If You Love Your Job

Fraser, T.M. "Human Stress, Work and Job Satisfaction," *Occupations Safety and Health Series*, #50, International Labour Office, Geneva.

Gruneberg, Michael M. *Understanding Job Satisfaction*. Macmillan, 1979.

Ivancevich, John M. and Michael T. Matteson. *Organizational Behavior and Management*. Business Publications, Inc., Plano, Texas.

The Business Coach

Bendaly, Leslie. *Strength in Numbers*. McGraw-Hill Ryerson, 1990.

Connor, Dennis with Edward Clatlin. *The Art of Winning*. St. Martin's Press, 1988.

Stern, Paul G. with Tom Shachtman. *Straight to the Top*. Warner Books, 1991.

Messy Desks

Booher, Dianna. *Cutting Paperwork in the Corporate Culture*. Facts on File Publications, 1986.

Mayer, Jeffrey J. *If You haven't Got the Time to Do It Right, When Will You Find the Time to Do It Over?* Simon & Schuster, 1990.

Myers, Rochelle and Michael Ray. *Creativity in Business*. Doubleday, 1986.

The Joys of Sponsorship

Bergin, Ron. *Sponsorship & the Arts: A Guide to Corporate Sponsorship of the Performing & Visual Arts*. Entertainment Resource Group, 1990.

Lant, Jeffrey, M.D. *Development Today—A Fundraising Guide for Nonprofit Organizations*. JLA Publications, 1980 (revised 1986).

Young, Joyce. *Fundraising for Nonprofit Groups: How to get money from corporations, foundations and government*. International Self-Counsel Press, 1978 (revised 1989).

Common Scents

Jackson, Judith. *Scentual Touch*. Ballantine, 1987.

Rechelbacher, Horst. *Rejuvenation*. Inner Traditions International, 1987.

Tisserand, Robert B. *The Art of Aromatherapy*. Inner Traditions International, 1977.

Protection of Intellectual Property

Dohlman, Ebba, "International Piracy and Intellectual Property," *The OECD Observer*, October-November 1988.

"Innovation and Intellectual Property Rights in Canada," Science Council of Canada, Ottawa.

"Lock Up Your Software, "*The Economist*, January 14, 1989, p. B9.

United Kingdom University Directors of Industrial Liaison,"University Intellectual Property: Its Management and Commercial Exploitation," *International Journal of Technology Management* 1989 4:5, pp. 563-585.

Your Public Face

Campbell, Andrew. *One Step Ahead: Keeping Your Company Competitive*. McGraw-Hill Ryerson, 1989.

Mackay, Harvey. *Swim With the Sharks*. William Morrow, 1988.

McDonald, James. *Management Without Tears*. Crain Books, 1981.

Retrophobia

Levi, Lennart, M.D. *Preventing Work Stress*. Addison-Wesley, 1981.

Bansabel, Jane, Alfred Godloe, and John Kelly. *Managing Yourself*. Franklin Watts, 1984.

Hoover-Dempsey, Kathleen, Ph.D., and Jeanne Plas, Ph.D. *Working Up a Storm*. W.W. Norton, 1988.

The Write Stuff

Block, Mervin. *Writing Broadcast News—Shorter, Sharper, Stronger*. Bonus Books, 1987.

Fiske, Robert Hartwell. *Guide to Concrete Writing*. Simon & Schuster, 1990.

Zinsser, William. *On Writing Well*. Harper Collins, 1990.

Personal and Business Ethics

Guy, Mary E. *Ethical Decision Making in Everyday Work Situations*. Greenwood, 1990.

Siolos, Anna M. *An Ethics Primer for Children. Honesty—Kindness—Respect: A Catalyst to Discussion*. Agatha, 1989.

Taylor, Barbara Ley. *Managers Talk Ethics*. John Wiley & Sons, 1991.

Taylor, Paul W. *Principles of Ethics: An Introduction*. Wadsworth, 1975.

Committees That Work

Parr, Jim. *Any Other Business*. Clarke, Irwin, 1977.

Pohl, Alice N. *Committees and Boards: How to be an effective participant*. NTC Business Books, 1990.

Sheppard, John Ben. *The President's Guide to Club and Organization Management and Meetings*. Hawthorne, 1960.

Reading the Customer

Anderson, Kristen and Ron Zemke. *Delivering Knock Your Socks Off Service*. American Management Association, 1991.

Davidson, William H. and Bro Uttal. *Total Customer Service*. Harper and Row, 1988.

Lele, Miland M. with Jagdish N. Sheth. *The Customer Is Key*. John Wiley & Sons, 1991.

Solomon, Muriel. *Working With Difficult People*. Prentice-Hall, 1991.

Creative Complaining

Bower, Sharon Anthony and Gordon H. Bower. *Asserting Yourself*. Addison-Wesley, 1991.

Bramson, Robert M. *Coping With Difficult People*. Dell, 1981.

Edmonston, Phil. *The Art of Complaining*. General, 1988.

HEALTH'S WEALTH

Eating and Stress

Chapman, G.E. and C.E. Greenwood, "Diet, Brain and Behavior: Implications for Stress Management," *Nutrition Quarterly*, Vol. XI, pp 9-13.

Stoltz, Sandra Gordon. *The Food Fix: A recovery guide for destructive eaters.* Prentice-Hall, 1983.

Wurtman, Judith J., Ph.D. *Managing Your Mind and Mood Through Food.* Harper Collins, 1988.

The Great Killer

Feuer, Louis C. *White Collar Stress.* Frederick Fell/Book Center Inc., 1987.

Gordon, Thomas, M.D. *Lead Effectiveness Training.* Wyden/Bantam, 1978.

Kopp, Sheldon. *Raise Your Right Hand Against Fear.* CompCare Publishers, 1988.

Peurifoy, Reneau Z. *Anxiety, Phobias, and Panic.* Lifeskills, 1988.

Counting Sheep

Ellis, Keith. *How to Cope With Insomnia.* Heinemann, 1983.

Hales, Dianne. *How to Sleep Like a Baby.* Ballantine, 1987.

Lambley, Peter, M.D. *Insomnia and Other Sleep Problems.* Pinnacle, 1985.

Take a Walk

Jonas, Steve, M.C., and Peter Radetsky. *Pace Walking.* Crown, 1988.

Kashiwa, Anne and James Rippe, M.D. *Fitness Walking for Women.* Putman, 1987.

Kunzleman, Charles T. *The Complete Book of Walking.* Simon & Schuster, 1979.

Health Protection in the Tropics

Gyorkos, T. and P. Viens. *The Tropical Traveller.* Hobbit Software Inc., Montreal.

Drinking Water Away From Home. Health Directorate, Health Protection Branch, Health and Welfare Canada.

Stewart, Gordon W. *Things Your Travel Agent Never Told You: A traveler's survival guide to health, fitness and worry-free travel.* Grosvenor House, 1983.

Eating Out Well and Healthily

Brody, Jane. *Jane Brody's Good Food Book: Living the High-Carbohydrate Way.* Bantam, 1987.

Lindsay, Anne. *The Lighthearted Cookbook.* Key Porter Books Ltd., 1988.

Perl, Lila. *Junk Food, Fast Food, Health Food: What America eats and why.* Houghton Mifflin/Clarion Books, 1980.

Sick of Being Tired

Chaitow, Leon. *The Beat Fatigue Workbook.* Thorsons Publishing Group, 1988.

Earle, Richard, Ph.D., and David Imrie, M.D., with Rick Archbold. *Your Vitality Quotient.* Fawcett Crest, 1990.

Gardner, David C., M.D., and Grace J. Beatty, M.D. *Never Be Tired Again!* Rawson Associates, 1988.

Sitting Fit

DeCarlo, Thomas J. *The Executive's Handbook of Balanced Physical Fitness.* Association Press, 1975.

Parker, Barbara. *Sit Down, Shape Up.* Leisure Press, 1983.

Prevention magazine. *Fitness for Everyone.* Rodale Press, 1984.

The "Sweet Restorer"

Lamberg, Lynne. *Better Sleep.* Random House, 1984.

Maxmen, Jerrold S., M.D. *A Good Night's Sleep.* Norton, 1981.

Regestein, Quentin, M.D., and David Ritchie. *Sleep: Problems and Solutions.* Consumers Union, 1990.

Swimming for Health and Pleasure

Brems, Marianne. *The Fit Swimmer, 120 Workouts and Training Tips.* Contemporary Books, 1984.

Wagenvoord, James S. *The Swim Book..* Bobbs-Merrill, 1980.

A Laugh a Day

Burton, Robert. *The Anatomy of Melancholy.* Tudor Publishing, 1941.

Cousins, Norman. *Anatomy of an Illness as Perceived by the Patient: Reflections on Healing and Regeneration.* W.W. Norton, 1979.

Moody, Raymond A., Jr., M.D. *Laugh After Laugh.* Headwater Press, 1978.

Couch Potatoes

Bricklin, Mark. *Lose Weight Naturally*. Rodale Press, 1989.

Parker, Barbara. *Sit Down, Shape Up*. Leisure Press, 1983.

In addition to the two books listed above, we suggest "Jacki Sorensen's Aerobic Dancing 'Encore'," for beginners. Also, "Every Day with Richard Simmons Family Fitness."

That Awful Cold

Brody, Jane. *The New York Times Guide to Personal Health*. Avon, 1983.

Health News. The University of Toronto Faculty of Medicine monthly guide to current Health Issues, December 1987 and December 1988.

Miller, Penny F., B.Sc., Pharm M.A., "Remedies for Common Cold Symptoms," *Canadian Family Physician*, January 1991.

Fares of the Heart

Hamilton, Eva May Nunnelley and Eleanor Noss Whitney. *Nutrition: Concepts and Controversies*. West Publishing, 1982.

Katch, Frank I. and William D. McArdle. *Nutrition, Weight Control and Exercise*. Lea and Febiger, 1983.

Watson, Julie. *Heart Smart Cooking on a Shoestring*. Macmillan, 1991.

Coping With Depression

Bailey, Linda J. *How to Get Going When You Can Barely Get Out of Bed*. Prentice-Hall, 1983.

Cleve, Jay, M.D. *Out of the Blues*. CompCare Publishers, 1989.

Gold, Mark S., M.D. *The Good News About Depression*. Villard Books, 1987.

KNOWING THYSELF

The Time of Our Lives

Douglas, Merril E. and Donna Douglas. *Manage Your Time, Manage Your Work, Manage Yourself*. American Management Association, 1980.

Fiore, Neil. *The Now Habit*. Jeremy P. Tarcher, 1989.

McCrae, Bradley. *Practical Time Management: How to do More Things in Less Time*. International Self-Counsel Press, 1988.

Shed a Tear

Callwood, June. *Emotions*. Doubleday, 1986.

Daniels, Victor and Lawrence J. Horowitz. *Being and Caring*. San Francisco Book Company, 1976.

Haldane, Sean. *Emotional First Aid*. New Horizons Press, 1984.

Ornstein, Robert and David Sobel. *Healthy Pleasures*. Addison Wesley, 1989.

Temper, Temper!

Gaylin, Willard. *The Rage Within*. Penguin, 1989.

Lerner, Harriet Goldhar, Ph.D. *The Dance of Anger*. Harper & Row, 1985.

Ravris, Carol. *Anger: The Misunderstood Emotion*. Simon & Schuster, 1984.

Reading People

Cherney, Marcia B. and Susan A. Tynan with Ruth Duskin Feldman. *Communicoding*. Donald I. Fine, 1989.

Murphy, Kevin J. *Effective Listening*. Bantam, 1987.

Walton, Donald. *Are You Communicating?* McGraw-Hill, 1989.

The Big Five-O

Donohugh, Donald L., M.D. *The Middle Years*. Saunders, 1981.

Pruner, Morton. *Getting the Most Out of Your Fifties*. Crown, 1977.

Schuckman, Terry. *Aging is Not For Sissies*. Westminster, 1975.

Disabilities—Theirs & Ours

Galbreaith, Patricia. *What You Can Do For Yourself: Hints for the Handicapped*. Drake Publishers Inc., 1974.

Griffin, John Howard. *Black Like Me*. NAL Dutton, 1962.

Rogers, Michael A. *Living With Paraplegia*. Faber and Faber, 1986.

Outside Interests

Jackson, Donald. *The Story of Writing*. Taplinger Publishing Co., 1981.

Needham, Jack. *Modelling Ships in Bottles*. Patrick Stephens Ltd., 1988.

Voss, Gunther. *Reinhold Craft and Hobby Book*. Reinhold Publishing Corp., 1963.

You Too Can Be Creative

Gregory, Carl E. *The Management of Intelligence: Scientific problem solving and creativity.* McGraw-Hill, 1967.

van Oech, Roger. Illustrated by George Willett. *A Whack on the Side of the Head: How to unlock your mind for innovation.* Warner Books, 1990.

Prince, George M. *The Practice of Creativity.* Collier Books, 1972.

Old Dogs, New Tricks

Apps, Jerrold W. *Study skills for Adults Returning to School.* McGraw-Hill, 1982.

Cunningham, Phyllis M. and Sharon B. Merriam, Eds. *Handbook of Adult and Continuing Education.* Jossey-Bass Publishers, 1989.

Darkenwald, Gordon G. and Sharan B. Merriam. *Adult Education—Foundations of Practice.* Harper & Row, 1982.

Promises, Promises

Covey, Stephen R. *The Seven Habits of Highly Effective People.* Simon & Schuster, 1990.

Edman, Paul. *Why Kids Lie.* Penguin, 1989.

Townsend, Robert. *Up the Organization and Further Up the Organization.* Knopf, 1970.

Did You Forget?

Brothers, Joyce, Ph.D. *Ten Days to a Successful Memory.* Prentice-Hall, 1957.

Lorayne, Harry. *Harry Lorayne's Page-a-Minute Memory Book.* Holt Rinehart & Winston, 1985.

Miller, Emmett E., M.D. *Software for the Mind.* Celestial Arts, 1987.

Spirit of Imagination

Bosnak, Robert. *A Little Course in Dreams.* Shambhala Press, 1988.

Egan, Kieran and Dan Nadaner, Eds. *Imagination and Education.* Columbia University Teachers College Press, 1987.

Murdock, Maureen. *Spinning Inward.* Shambhala Press, 1987.

Voicing Success

Hoffman, William C. *The Speaker's Notebook.* McGraw-Hill, 1943.

Micalie, Paul. *Shortcuts to Impressive Speaking.* Hawthorn Books, 1975.

Wilder, Lilyan. *Talk Your Way to Success.* Simon & Schuster, 1986.

Styles of Learning

Brookfield, Stephen D. *The Skilful Teacher*. Jossey-Bass Publishers, 1990.

Kolb, David A. *The Learning Style Inventory: Technical Manual*. McBer, 1976.

Macrorie, Ken. *Twenty Teachers*. Oxford University Press, 1984.

The Joys of Solitude

Freeman, Lawrence, O.S.B. *The Light Within*. Crossroad Publishing, 1987.

Goldstein, Joan and Manuela Soares. *The Joy Within: A Beginner's Guide to Meditation*. Prentice Hall, 1990.

LeShan, Lawerence. *How to Meditate*. Little, Brown, 1974.

Rogers, Harold. *A Handful of Quietness*. Word, Inc., 1977.

The Ties That Blind

von Fürstenberg, Egon. *The Power Look*. Holt, Rinehart and Winston, 1978.

McGill, Leonard. *Stylewise*. G.P. Putnam's Sons, 1983.

Pinckney, Gerrie and Marge Swenson. *New Image for Men*. Reston Publishing, 1983.

What to Do?

Donaldson, Gordon and Jay W. Lorsch. *Decision Making at the Top*. Basic Books, 1983.

Prince, George M. *The Practice of Creativity*. Harper & Row, 1970.

Russo, J. Edward and Paul J.H. Schoemaker. *Decision Traps: The ten barriers to brilliant decision-making and how to overcome them*. Doubleday, 1989.

So Much To Read

Davies, Robertson. *A Voice From the Attic*. Viking, 1960.

Fadiman, Clifton. *The Lifetime Reading Plan*. World, 1960.

Roseberg, Betty. *Genreflecting*. Libraries Unlimited, 1986.

Relaxing Your Mind

Flesch, Rudolf. *The Art of Clear Thinking*. Harper & Row, 1951.

Mitchell, Richard. *Less Than Words Can Say*. Little Brown, 1979.

Rogers, Harold. *A Handful of Quietness*. Word, Inc., 1977.

Self-Esteem at Any Age

Branden, Nathaniel. *The Psychology of Self-Esteem*. Bantam, 1969.

Meacham, Daniel. *The Magic of Self-Confidence*. Simon & Schuster, 1984.

Write Down Those Goals

Chilton, David. *The Wealthy Barber*. Stoddart, 1989.

Covey, Stephen R. *Principle-Centred Leadership*. Summit, 1991.

Youngs, Bettie B. *Goal-Setting Skills for Young People*. Bilicki Publications, 1989.

The Uses of Prophecy

Anthony, Robert, M.D. *Do What You Love, Loving What You Do*. Berkely, 1991.

Faber, Adele and Elaine Mazlish. *How to Talk So Kids Will Listen and Listen So Kids Will Talk*. Avon, 1980.

Phillips, Debora, M.D. with Fred Bernstein. *How to Give Your Child a Great Self-Image*. Penguin, 1989.

The Mystery of Confidence

Bennies, Warren. *On Becoming a Leader*. Addison-Wesley, 1989.

Carnegie, Dale. *How to Develop Self-Confidence and Influence People by Public Speaking*. Pocket Books, 1923.

Cox, Allan. *The Achiever's Profile*. American Management Association, 1988.

FAMILY TIES

Superb Teachers

Hentoff, Nat. *Does Anybody Give a Damn?* Alfred A. Knopf, 1977.

McLaren, Peter. *Cries From The Corridor*. Methuen, 1980.

Nathan, Joe. *Free To Teach*. The Pilgrim Press, 1983.

Rothman, Esther P. *Troubled Teachers*. David McKay Company Inc., 1977.

Time At Home

Crandall, Elizabeth W., Irma H. Gross, and Marjorie M. Knoll. *Management for Modern Families*. Prentice-Hall, 1980.

Hersh, S.P., M.D. *The Executive Parent*. Sovereign Books, 1975.

Winston, Stephanie. *Getting Organized*. W.W. Norton, 1978.

You & Your Parents

Halpern, Howard M., Ph.D. *Cutting Loose*. Simon & Schuster, 1976.

MacLean, Helene. *Caring For Your Parents*. Doubleday, 1987.

Teresi, Jeanne and Marcella Bakur Weiner with Corrine Stretch. *Old People Are a Burden, But Not My Parents*. Prentice-Hall, 1983.

Your Underachieving Child

Butler-Por, Nava. *Underachievers in School*. John Wiley & Sons, 1987.

Mandel, Harvey, M.D. *The Psychology of Underachievement*. John Wiley & Sons, 1988.

Rimm, Sylvia, M.D. *The Underachievement Syndrome*. Apple Publications, 1986.

Safety in the Home

Brown, Tom, Jr. with Brandt Morgan. *Tom Brown's Field Guide to City and Suburban Survival*. Berkeley Books, 1984.

Kerner, Fred. *The M&S Home Emergency Handbook & First-Aid Guide*. McClelland & Stewart, 1990.

Smith, Bradley and Gus Stevens. *The Emergency Book*. Simon & Schuster, 1978.

The State of Your Union

Napier, Augustus Y., Ph.D. *The Fragile Bond*. Harper & Row, 1988.

Richardson, Ronald W., M.D. *Family Ties that Bind*. Self-Counsel Press, 1989.

Rubin, Jeffrey, M.D. and Carol Rubin, M.D. *When Families Fight*. William Morrow, 1989.

Full-time Parents at Home

Bradman, Tony. *The Essential Father*. Unwin Paperbacks, 1985.

Ehrensaft, Dianne. *Parenting Together*. University of Illinois Press, 1990.

Queenan, John T., M.D., and Carrie N. Queenan, Eds. *A New Life: Pregnancy, Birth, and Your Child's First Year*. General Publishing, 1986.

Women in Canada. Statistical Report 1990, from Statistics Canada 1990, Statistics Canada 1989, 503.

Summer Camps

Ball, Armand and Beverly Ball. *Basic Camp Management*. American Camping Association, 1990.

New York Times Magazine. Supplement published weekly in *The New York Times* Sunday edition.

Silvert, Sheldon and Jeremy Solomon. *The Parent's Guide to Summer Camp.* Farrar, Straus & Giroux, 1991.

The Sandwich Generation

Cohen, Stephen Z., M.D. and Bruce M. Gans. *The Other Generation Gap.* Dodd, Mead, 1988.

Rhodes, Ann. *Caring for the Elderly.* Grosvenor House, 1989.

Richardson, Ronald W., M.D. *Family Ties That Bind.* Self-counsel Press, 1989.

The Inestimable Value of Pets

Wyatt, Valerie. *Everything You Want to Know About Pets.* Greey de Pencier, 1988.

Katz, Sidney, "How Pets Help People," *Chatelaine,* December 1985, pp. 114, 118, 120.

Messmann, Jon. *Choosing a Pet.* Grosset & Dunlap, 1973.

Mitchener, Kathy L., M.D., "The Human Animal Bond and the Practicing Veterinarian," *Companion Animal Practice,* Vol. 2, No. 4, April 1988, pp. 3-5.

Pearce, Susan, "The Bond," *Dogs in Canada Annual,* 1991, pp. 19-23, 201.

Printed in Canada